Many Languages, Building Connections:

Supporting Infants and Toddlers Who Are Dual Language Learners

by Karen Nemeth

Acknowledgment

Gratitude and admiration to Linda Groves Gillespie for her helpful input on this project and for sharing her infant/toddler magic over the years, and to my editor, Laura Laxton, for a great collaboration!

Also by Karen Nemeth:

Many Languages, One Classroom:

Teaching Dual and English Language Learners

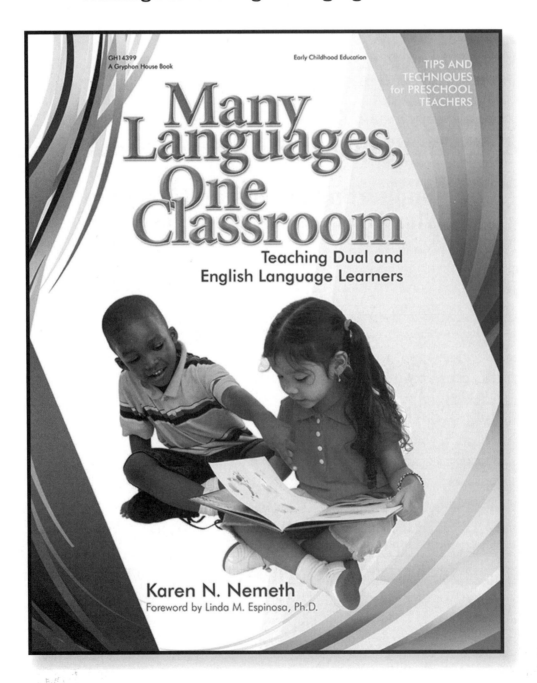

Many Languages, Building Connections

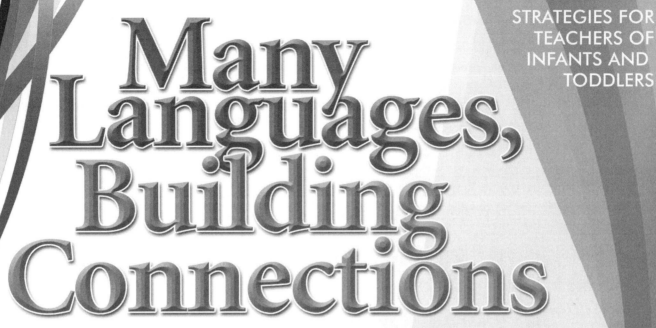

Supporting Infants and Toddlers Who Are Dual Language Learners

Karen N. Nemeth

Gryphon House, Inc.
Lewisville, NC

© 2012 Karen Nemeth

Published by Gryphon House, Inc.

PO Box 10, Lewisville, NC 27023

800-638-0928; 877-638-7576 (fax)

Visit us on the web at www.gryphonhouse.com.

Library of Congress Cataloging-in-Publication Data

Nemeth, Karen N.

   Many languages, building connections : supporting infants and toddlers who are dual language learners / Karen N. Nemeth.

     p. cm.

  ISBN 978-0-87659-389-9 (pbk.)

1. English language--Study and teaching (Preschool)--United States--Foreign speakers. 2. Native language--Study and teaching (Preschool)--United States. 3. Second language acquisition--United States. 4. Education, Bilingual--United States. 5. Education, Preschool--United States. I. Title.

  PE1128.A2N37355 2012

  428.2'4--dc23

                           2011049903

BULK PURCHASE

Gryphon House books are available for special premiums and sales promotions as well as for fund-raising use. Special editions or book excerpts also can be created to specifications. For details, contact the Director of Marketing at Gryphon House.

DISCLAIMER

Gryphon House, Inc. cannot be held responsible for damage, mishap, or injury incurred during the use of or because of activities in this book. Appropriate and reasonable caution and adult supervision of children involved in activities and corresponding to the age and capability of each child involved is recommended at all times. Do not leave children unattended at any time. Observe safety and caution at all times.

Reprinted May 2018

Table of Contents

CHAPTER

1 Introduction

Why do you need this book?

**FOCUS
QUESTIONS**

- What do you expect to learn from this book?

- What challenges are you facing that you hope will be addressed in this book?

Thirteen-month-old Kayla said, "Bah!" and reached toward the basket. Her caregiver knew what she was asking for and handed Kayla the ball from the basket, repeating and expanding: "Ball! You said ball! You want the ball? Here it is!" Kayla bounced excitedly in her seat.

Meanwhile, 11-month-old José said, "Po!" and reached toward the basket. His caregiver responded with, "Po. Isn't it cute you are trying to make little noises." She smiled and repeated, "Po," then turned to play with Kayla and the ball. José got quiet and turned away. Unfortunately, his caregiver did not realize he, too, was trying to say the word ball *but in his home language. If she had known that* pelota *meant "ball," she might have responded differently.*

Caring for someone else's baby is an awesome and wonderful responsibility. Getting to know each tiny new person with his unique characteristics and personality, his likes and dislikes, and his family and culture is fascinating. Caregivers today are witnessing rapidly increasing diversity, which brings a critical question into focus: What is the best way to care for an infant or toddler who comes from a language background different from your own?

So much has been written about language education, ESL (English as a second language), and bilingual education for K–12 teachers, and we've seen a bloom of books written about teaching preschool children who are dual language learners. However, none of these resources gets to the heart of what infant and toddler caregivers want and need to know. The goal of this book is to help any adult caring for a baby or toddler to feel confident that he knows how language develops, how cultural differences can come into play, and how to assess an individual child's situation to provide appropriate supports.

The 2010 U.S. Census estimates that about 25 percent of children younger than the age of six are born to immigrant families, making this the fastest-growing segment of our population (Fortuny, Hernandez, and Chaudry, 2010). Infants and toddlers whose families speak many different languages are appearing in all kinds of early care and learning settings in growing numbers. These infants and toddlers may receive care at home, in someone else's home, or in a center. They may have large extended families or live with just one parent. They may live in wealthy homes full of expensive toys and furnishings or in homes with little to offer the growing mind of a young child. They may be seen by doctors, dentists, therapists, social workers, and nurses, or they may be in situations with few services. They may be thriving in secure homes or struggling in stressful environments. They may be growing up with two languages or more.

The more we learn about how important support for the home language and culture is to building a strong foundation for literacy, self-esteem, and relationships, the more we realize this support must extend to all children, even the very youngest. A rich cultural and linguistic heritage provides many advantages. Parents and caregivers need to share a common understanding and vision for raising young children whose home language is not English.

We know that language is a vital component of early experiences well before a child can say his first word. We cannot afford to wait until children get to elementary school to start addressing the development of their home languages and their learning of English. Yet, most professional-development programs for infant/toddler teachers do not introduce strategies for supporting linguistic and cultural differences for the youngest children. Nor do most programs for ESL and general-education teachers address the care of infants and toddlers from different language and cultural backgrounds. In this book, both professors and professional-development providers will find ways to enhance their classes so they can better prepare caregivers for the diverse reality they will encounter in their work.

In addition, home visitors, family child-care monitors, program directors, trainers, nannies, consultants, therapists, early intervention specialists, pediatricians, social workers, and other early childhood professionals need knowledge and strategies to support the development of babies in bilingual environments with unique cultural traditions. All adults who have responsibilities for children younger than the age of three can help form nurturing communities to enhance the infants' and toddlers' experiences, including their experiences with culture and language.

Several terms are used to describe children who are growing up with two or more languages, and the programs that serve them. The term we use in this book is *dual language learners*, or DLLs, because it is currently the term of choice for key national organizations such as the Office of Head Start (which oversees Early Head Start programs for infants and toddlers); the Council for Exceptional Children, Division for Early Childhood; and Zero to Three, the national professional organization for infant/toddler caregivers and parents.

In each chapter of the book, you will find focus questions to guide your reading, as well as reflection questions to help clarify your thoughts, feelings, and knowledge. These questions can be used by the individual reader to get the most out of the material, or they can serve as tools to support and document professional learning, staff discussions, and training events.

- What are goals that everyone might agree on for young children in their first three years?

- Are these goals affected by the children's culture or the adult's culture?

Interesting questions, indeed! If you ask people to answer quickly, you may hear very similar answers; however, when given time to explain their responses, people reveal subtle and significant variations. What do we want for infants and toddlers? For example, we want them to grow up in a safe and clean environment, but not too safe so they never face challenges (and it is this level of safety that causes disagreements). Some states regulate that it is absolutely unsafe for one adult to care for more than two infants, while other states find it acceptable to care for three or four without help. We also do not want the environment too clean, as recent studies say that exposing young children to very few germs in infancy may not be the best way to help them develop key immunities. But how clean is too clean? Is this a practical question or a cultural one? It is probably a bit of both.

We can agree that we all want children to grow up nurtured and loved, but how do we show that love? In the United States, many mothers practice "attachment parenting" and wear their babies in slings against their bodies all the time. Other mothers find that terribly restrictive and believe it is more loving to allow the child his independence so he can develop self-regulation and a separate identity. Practical or cultural?

We certainly want children to grow up with the ability to take care of themselves. American programs place strong emphasis on getting infants to feed themselves and dress themselves as early as possible, but other cultures view these self-help skills as less important than the bonding that takes place between caregiver and child. Are the people from those other cultures any less able to dress themselves as adults? Practical or cultural?

Our assumptions can really get in the way as we work toward providing culturally and linguistically responsive care for infants and toddlers. Taking the time to develop an awareness of your own culturally based assumptions will help you open up to the value of learning the variations in the goals people have for young children. There is no one right way to love a child. There are, however, several basic guiding principles that will be upheld throughout this book.

Basic Guiding Principles

1. Every baby needs the security and comfort provided by the bond with the people who love him most. The job of the caregiver is to enter into that bond, support it, and enhance it with her own special presence. The best way to do this is for the caregiver to share the language of love that the baby has started or grown up with.

2. Every parent has a unique way of bringing up her baby, based on a combination of personality, experiences, preferences, knowledge, and culture. And every caregiver brings a unique style, based on all these factors as well. It is not a competition of who is "right." The goal should be to understand each other and keep an open mind, blending all these elements into a rich, warm, responsive dance of love for the baby.

3. Every baby needs to hear some talk, stories, play, and singing in his home language every day. If that language is not English, then he will benefit from having those experiences in English every day as well. Caregivers and families need to work together to make sure infants and toddlers get rich, correct, engaging input in both languages.

4. Being bilingual is good for all children, not just the ones who happen to come from a non-English-speaking family! All caregivers should consider adopting this goal and making it a reality.

5. Language acquisition is more than just learning vocabulary. It is a complex and sophisticated developmental process in which the brain depends on strong, responsive, nurturing relationships to make sense of everything it learns about the world. The brain connects words to ideas. This process has to be supported by people during the critical first two years of a child's life.

6. Language is embedded in culture; the two are intertwined.

7. Language, identity, and self-esteem are also interlaced. For each of us, our language is part of who we are. For infants and toddlers, language is an inseparable part of who their parents are as well.

All infants and toddlers need experiences that nurture, support, and teach their home language and culture. Research has shown the importance of this foundation as a contributor to potential success in English. Even for babies, we should remember that full immersion in an English-only program that reduces their home language will not offer any learning or developmental advantages (August and Shanahan, 2006).

Of course, our concerns go beyond just worrying about how a child will succeed in school. We keep in mind this important insight from noted researcher Lilly Wong Fillmore (1991):

When parents are unable to talk to their children, they cannot easily convey to them their values, beliefs, understandings, or wisdom about how to cope with their experiences. They cannot teach them about the meaning of work, or about personal responsibility, or what it means to be a moral or ethical person in a world with too many choices and too few guideposts to follow. What is lost are the bits of advice, the consejos parents should be able to offer children in their everyday interactions with them. Talk is a crucial link between parents and children: It is how parents impart their cultures to their children and enable them to become the kind of men and women they want them to be. When parents lose the means for socializing and influencing their children, rifts develop and families lose the intimacy that comes from shared beliefs and understandings.

Planning Chart

What are your greatest challenges and concerns about meeting the needs of diverse infants and toddlers and their families? Fill out the planning chart on page 107 to help identify your needs, then look for answers throughout the book.

CHAPTER 2

Using This Book in Different Infant and Toddler Care Settings

Where will we find culturally and linguistically diverse infants and toddlers?

FOCUS QUESTIONS

- What are the different types of settings where someone other than parents may care for an infant who speaks a different language?

- What do we need to know to make sure each one of those settings provides the best environment for an infant or toddler with different language needs and cultural background?

Infant and toddler care options are not all created equal. Quite a few possibilities exist, and each one comes with its own questions and challenges for meeting the needs of infants and toddlers from different language backgrounds. Following are brief summaries of the most common options.

Child Care Center

In this group care setting, the infant or toddler is usually in a room with a small number of other children of similar age, and a teacher, or a teacher and an assistant. Ideally, each child will have a primary caregiver who can bond with that particular baby and meet her needs in the best possible way. At the very least, we would hope to see infants and toddlers cared for in small groups with consistent caregivers. However, staff turnover and absenteeism with substitutes might mean a lot of changing relationships for a baby.

Because this is the critical period for language development in both first and second languages, it is imperative that center-based programs make sure all their staff members receive training for supporting both languages. Centers also need to find creative ways to stay actively in touch with parents, even when the demands of their busy lives make it seem that parents just rush in and out of the building.

Language-Immersion and Language-Teaching Programs

Language-immersion programs provide some level of classroom experience. Examples include a one-day-per-week "mommy and me" class, an instructor who visits children in the local child care center, or a part-time program toddlers might attend to be briefly immersed in another language. Some of these programs are based on programs for older children, watered down, and presented for infants and toddlers. Others provide more developmentally appropriate learning activities that depend on strong partnerships with parents. Be aware that research has clearly shown (Kuhl, 2010) that audio recordings and videos by themselves do nothing to teach infants and toddlers any language. Parents should look for language programs that use hands-on, play-based techniques with authentic, functional, and communicative language activities.

Remember, though, that even a wonderful language program built around the children's needs and interests, with stories, songs, and movement, should not be too strict regarding the use of languages. There may be times when it is important to support the child in whatever language she needs to use to make a connection.

Family or Home Child Care

Most states have rules regarding the operation of child care services in someone's home. The regulations regarding group size and qualifications vary widely from state to state. In some states, though, it is perfectly legal to operate family child care in your home with no requirements or monitoring at all. In other states, family child care providers have access to extensive professional development.

A provider who speaks only one language but cares for children who speak different languages needs support so she can learn some of the home languages of the children in her care. Bilingual providers should have professional development to help them use their language assets in the most effective way with the children in their care.

Early Head Start

EHS is not a child care program. It is a federally funded, community-based program designed to support the families of children younger than the age of three. This support reaches children early enough to make a difference in their ability to succeed in school. EHS may serve children via home visits, visits to family child care homes, or center-based programming. The Office of Head Start has provided increasing amounts of support and information for anyone involved in these settings who cares for babies whose language is not English (see http://eclkc.ohs.acf.hhs.gov/hslc).

Home Visiting Services

Although babies living in their own homes with their families do not present diversity as we see it in group settings, this does not mean there are no language issues in the home. Home visitors, who are often nurses or former teachers, need to understand the importance of helping family members contribute to the child's early literacy by reading aloud, singing, and playing games in their home language. Many home-visitor programs have not focused on helping families support continued development in the home language. However, these home visitors can be of critical importance in encouraging the kind of home-language support young DLLs really need. Home visitors' training and professional development should include information on the language development of dual language learners.

Early Intervention

A child with a condition or special need who is identified as needing services from early intervention will have an Individual Family Services Plan (IFSP). This written document details what special services the young child and her family will receive. This might mean that a specialist or therapist will come to the baby's house or place of care for a certain number of hours per week to show the parents and caregivers how to work with the child to alleviate physical, cognitive, or language-development issues. The majority of early intervention team members have not had any training regarding the language development and needs of dual language learners. Two critical resources they should receive are the Council for Exceptional Children, Division for Early Childhood (CEC-DEC) position statement, *Responsiveness to ALL Children, Families, and Professionals: Integrating Cultural and Linguistic Diversity into Policy and Practice* (2010), and the newest edition of *Dual Language Development and Disorders* (Paradis, Genesee, and Crago, 2010).

Some therapists, doctors, and early intervention specialists still harbor the unfounded belief that children with early speech or language delays should not be exposed to two languages. Not only is this completely untrue, but young children who face language challenges benefit from continuing support for their home language, in addition to support in developing the language they will need in school.

Nannies, Au Pairs, and Babysitters

Many families hire private in-home care providers who speak a language other than English to help their young children grow up with the advantage of being bilingual. This can be a positive and powerful experience, but there are some important factors to consider. Both the parents and the in-home care providers should understand the need for training and support to make sure the baby receives high-quality language support in both languages.

Family, Friend, and Neighbor Care

Many times families will rely on relatives, neighbors, or friends to provide occasional or regularly scheduled care for their infant or toddler. Some prefer this situation to formal, center-based care, and others choose it for affordability. Because of the nature of the relationships in these situations, parents can have a hard time guiding the behavior of the caregiver. Still, when parents place their precious infant or toddler in someone else's care during the crucial language-learning period, they need to share what they know about using the home language with the baby even while also exposing her to English.

REFLECTION QUESTIONS

- Think of your own experiences as a young child or in finding care for your own infant. What kind of care are you familiar with? How do you feel about the pros and cons of these different types of infant/toddler care?

- What effective strategy do you remember from the care you experienced that you think would be effective with the DLLs in your care? What is a weak strategy that you have learned to avoid?

CHAPTER 3

What's New in the Language-Development Field?

What are the basics every caregiver needs to know?

FOCUS QUESTIONS

- How can we separate fact from myth about caring for infant and toddler DLLs?

- What do our national organizations contribute to the discussion regarding this care?

- What are the key components of early development that inform us on how best to meet the needs of young DLLs?

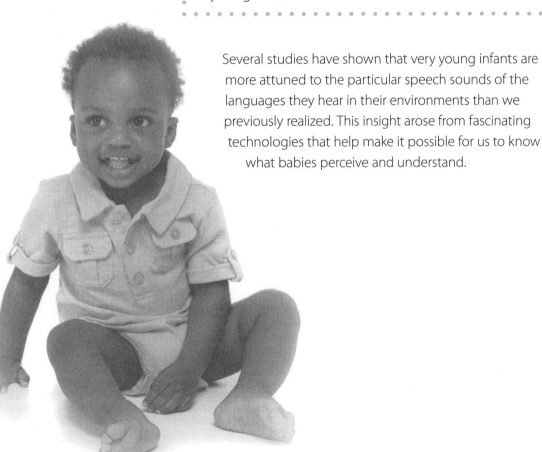

Several studies have shown that very young infants are more attuned to the particular speech sounds of the languages they hear in their environments than we previously realized. This insight arose from fascinating technologies that help make it possible for us to know what babies perceive and understand.

How to Read Research as a Critical Thinker

Research can be difficult. Research with infants and toddlers can be especially difficult. Scientists can observe them, but infants and toddlers can not tell us what is on their minds or fill in a survey or follow instructions. A variety of techniques—often using sophisticated scanning and observational technologies—have been developed to try to gain some insight into what happens in a baby's brain. But we must be careful not to overgeneralize or misinterpret the findings of these studies. The following pointers will help you be an informed reader of research.

- Read the title and the conclusion. These will usually tell you exactly what the research found—no more, no less.

- Look at the number of subjects. Is the conclusion based on what happens with a handful of infants, or were a large number of babies included in the study? What were the characteristics of those subjects? For example, a study of children from middle-class Spanish-speaking homes in the United States does not tell us what happens with infants in homes that speak other languages or homes with higher or lower socioeconomic status.

- What exactly was measured in the study? We should not assume that the conclusions of the study inform us of anything other than what was measured. A study that measures infants' perceptions of initial consonant sounds cannot be assumed to reveal all we need to know about how they perceive or learn all speech sounds. An assessment that was found to be valid in measuring the perception of initial consonant sounds cannot be assumed to be valid in measuring language proficiency or intelligence.

News on Language Development

Interest in language development, particularly bilingual language development, has grown in the past five years. This expanded interest shows us two things: first, that new techniques and technologies allow us to get closer to understanding what happens in babies' brains; and second, that the topic compels scientists, policy makers, bloggers, and journalists to write about it, because language development draws so much attention from professionals and the media.

The research findings have shown us several interesting things.

- Bilingual infants show signs of developing enhanced cognitive flexibility in addition to learning two languages.

- An infant as young as a few days old can recognize and show preference for the speech sounds used by his mother, and will ignore speech sounds that do not occur in his mother's language.

- Infants can recognize and catalog the sounds of two languages if their mothers are bilingual, and they show preference for the two languages they have heard, while tuning out the sounds of unfamiliar languages.

- Infants with monolingual parents can learn to recognize and categorize sounds in a second language if that language is presented during interactions with an adult who visits with the child regularly over a period of several weeks—but no learning happens when the second language is presented for the same amount of time by a video recording.

The increasing interest in the development and needs of young dual language learners has received strong support from national organizations. Several groups have provided position statements to help practitioners interpret and properly use the research information.

The Council for Exceptional Children, Division for Early Childhood (CEC-DEC) released its updated statement in September 2010: *Responsiveness to ALL Children, Families, and Professionals: Integrating Cultural and Linguistic Diversity into Policy and Practice*, which states:

Research confirms that immersing DLLs fully in English when they are still in the active process of learning their home language actually has negative ramifications such as the inability to communicate with parents and relatives, preference for English, and depressed academic and reading achievement in English in later school years.

Meanwhile, the National Association for the Education of Young Children's statement, *Where we stand on responding to cultural and linguistic diversity*, says:

Encourage home language and literacy development, knowing that this contributes to children's ability to acquire English language proficiency. Research confirms that bilingualism is an asset and an educational achievement. When children become proficient and literate in their home language, they transfer those skills to a second language.

To give our youngest children the best start in life, we all need to work toward a celebration of bilingualism and cultural diversity for all infants and toddlers. Let's take a look at the factors that can inform best practices as we work toward that goal.

Brain Development Basics

Connection is a critical theme underlying our understanding of how infant brains develop and how they develop language. Connections from one brain cell to another, making the brain stronger, more versatile, and more useful, are facilitated by the connections children make between one piece of information and another. These information connections should be multisensory and must be repeated, practiced, expanded, and experienced. Connections between children and the adults who care for and nurture them provide a powerful vehicle for learning. These interpersonal connections enable infants and adults to respond to each other, to understand each other, and to get what they need. And, as children grow, we must support them as they make appropriate *connections with each other.*

Paradis, Genesee, and Crago (2010) say that growing up bilingual gives children advantages in the cognitive system known as *executive function*, even from infancy. "One aspect of executive function that has been found to be key to success in school is self-regulation abilities. For example, it seems that bilingual children have more success in focusing on one task along with the ability to screen out distractions." The development of the brain can be supported and strengthened by the experiences of growing up with two languages.

Challenges, Challenges, Challenges

Caring for a child who comes from a different language background does present more challenges—in understanding the child, in meeting his needs, in knowing what to do, in dealing with his parents, and in understanding cultural differences. But stop and think about how many challenges the family who is new to this country and its language must face each day in every task they undertake. The children and families who challenge you the most tend to be the ones who need you the most—and who need you to be the very best you can be as a teacher, child-development expert, and family advocate.

How Much Time Does It Take to Be Bilingual?

Does a child have to hear two languages equally to become fully bilingual? According to Barbara Zurer Pearson, well-known author and expert on growing up bilingual, young children need to be exposed to a language about 40–60 percent of their day to grow up understanding and using that language. Other factors, such as the role of each person using each language in the child's life, may influence the effectiveness of the language input. This means that children who speak a minority language at home but hear English at school, at the park, at the doctor's office, and so forth, need support from their families to continue providing practice in the minority language at home so it does not begin to slip away. (More on this topic will be covered in a later chapter.)

REFLECTION QUESTIONS

- What was the most surprising thing you learned in this chapter? How can you find out more?

- What new resources will you share with your colleagues after reading this chapter?

Planning Form

Use the planning form on page 108 to list your professional-development goals for supporting dual language learners in your work, then check off the goals you have met as you read the chapters of this book.

CHAPTER 4

First- and Second-Language Development

How do infants develop receptive and expressive abilities in two or more languages?

FOCUS QUESTIONS

- How much of language development happens before a baby starts talking?

- What are some ways that infants communicate without words?

Anyone who has spent time with babies knows a lot about how language blooms from the time children are born. Because language development is such a critical focus in early development, a truly effective infant/toddler caregiver must become a language-development expert. Of course, babies develop language skills at their own pace, so there is lots of variability in this process, but we can describe how the sequence generally takes place.

Before birth:	Perception and cataloging of speech sounds
At birth:	Infants recognize the speech sounds used by their mothers and ignore other sounds
Birth–6 weeks:	Communicate mainly through crying and body language
6 weeks–6 months:	Cooing
6 months–9 months:	Babbling
9 months–12 months:	Echolalic babbling
12 months:	First word
12 months–18 months:	Speaks one word at a time (holophrastic speech), learns a few new words each week
18 months:	Begins to say two words together (telegraphic speech)
18 months–30 months:	Two-word sentences, then three words, then whole sentences; vocabulary growing rapidly with several new words every day

Research (Kuhl, 2010) has revealed that infants as young as a few days old can recognize speech sounds in their mothers' language, but they ignore speech sounds not in the language they heard while in the womb. The human brain is wired and ready to focus on speech and to catalog the sounds and meanings in its environment. As adults, we do not control an infant's language development, but our behavior can do a lot to encourage or stifle it.

In the first few weeks, when infants communicate mainly by crying, caregivers and parents need to listen carefully to the different types of cries so they can respond appropriately. This helps the infant fine-tune her efforts to communicate her needs as she learns that her cries get her what she wants.

In the first six months, when infants are cooing with mainly vowel sounds, we can observe them becoming interested in a particular sound and trying to practice it over and over again. Babies who come from different home languages generally can detect different speech sounds, but cooing sounds the same from one language to another. Responding to these early attempts to practice particular sounds helps both the adult and the baby understand each other better.

Even in these early weeks, infants show that they understand key components of language and communication. You may have noticed that a young infant seems to know how to hold a conversation. When you get close, she will make a sound, then quiet down and watch your face as you make a response. She will wait until you are quiet to make her sound again.

Around the age of six months, we start to see babies take more control over their vocalizations. They begin to use more consonant sounds. This is the point when babbling begins to sound different in different languages. For the first six months, the child's brain has focused on listening to the speech sounds in the environment and cataloging them. After the six-month mark, infants are more able to produce those sounds, and we see that they gradually focus on practicing sounds they hear in the language around them and weeding out the sounds not used by others in their world. Caregivers of infants from different home languages may start to notice that infants at this age sound different from each other when they babble. Echoing the sounds they make and talking to them in their home languages can help them make the connection between the language they hear at home and the language they hear from you.

As the baby gets closer to nine or ten months, she begins to master another vital part of communication: tone of voice. We call this phase *echolalic babbling* because, although they do not say any actual words, infants certainly sound as if they are saying something. A baby who wants something will raise the tone at the end of her vocalization—just like she is asking a question. A baby whose big brother just grabbed her toy away will not sound like the baby asking for something: You will know exactly how that baby feels about losing her toy by the angry or upset tone of her voice. At this stage, infants get a lot of practice in the act of purposeful communication as they develop the sound and rhythm and meanings associated with speech—all before they have said a word.

This is a fascinating time in early development. We can see that the young brain needs time to observe and practice each aspect of language and communication before the child is ready to speak. Around the age of 12 months, children generally say their first real word. This may be *mama* or *dada* or something entirely different, such as *cat*, for example. If you ask people to think back about the babies they have known, they will report other first words such as *ball*, *bottle*, *more*, or *up*. It really is amazing that babies can select the most interesting or useful words as their first. Just think about it: How many hundreds of times a day do babies hear the words *the* or *and*, yet those words are not among the first. How many times a day—and with such expression—do babies hear their own names? Yet that is not the first word they utter.

Babies know so much about vocabulary and about communication that they can focus on saying first words that are useful to them and that get them what they want. No amount of praise or bribery can change that. The motivation to communicate comes from within each child. The support and encouragement we provide is critical to keep that language development going and to allow each child to reach her maximum potential. When a child reaches this stage and begins to experiment with pronouncing and practicing words from her home language, it is so important to make sure that the caregivers can recognize and respond to those early attempts. If not, as in our story about José, those first powerful and vital steps in expressive language may go unrecognized and unsupported. If the caregivers are not fluent in the child's home

Babies know so much about vocabulary and about communication that they can focus on saying first words that are useful to them and that get them what they want.

language, they need to take steps to learn and use that language with the child. They also need to work closely with parents so they can identify the sounds and words the infant is attempting and find ways to respond and expand on those early communications.

If language is a car, the infant is in the driver's seat! She decides which direction the car will go and how fast, but the car can not go without an engine—and that's what caring, nurturing adults provide, power to the language car. And think of the words in the environment as the fuel. The more and better quality the fuel, the farther and faster the language car can go. But, no matter what the engine tries to do or what kind of fuel is provided, that language car will always go just as fast and as far as the driver wants and is able to drive it.

Once a baby begins to say her first words, we realize that each word is filled with meaning. Imagine a toddler came up to you and said, "Sock!" What would your response be? You might say, "Oh, you took off your sock," or "Oh, you want me to help you with your sock?" or "Did you flush your sock down the toilet again?" You might not be sure what she meant by that one word, but you know she had a sentence or phrase of meaning in mind when she said that one word. We call that *holophrastic speech* because one word seems to mean a whole phrase.

A toddler approaches Miss Cary. "Bok!" says little Nicki. "Do you want to read a book? OK, go get a book." But Nicki just looks at Miss Cary and repeats, "Bok. BOK!" "Oh! You want to play with the blocks?" Then Nicki toddles off happily to the block area, looking back to make sure her caregiver is following her.

Even though Nicki only communicates with one word, Miss Cary knows she understands full sentences, so she uses those sentences to expand on what Nicki has said to help with the communication—and it works! This is an important time for caregivers to expand their understanding of the child's home language so they can understand the full context of the child's one-word utterances and provide that all-important expansive response.

Have you noticed that a child needs several months of practice at one-word utterances before she is ready to put two words together? No matter how many times she says, "Hi!" and how many times she says, "Daddy," she will not say, "Hi, Daddy!" until she is developmentally ready—no matter how much you try to reward her. This is a part of the process controlled by that child in the driver's seat of that language car.

Two-word utterances start to appear closer to 18 months. We call that *telegraphic speech* because the baby does not just say the first two words of the sentence; she says the two most meaningful words together. So you don't hear toddlers saying, "the car," but you might hear them say, "big car," or "Mommy car." This reminds us of the days when people sent telegrams by paying for each word, so they used the fewest words possible.

When I change baby Sarah's diaper, she holds out her hand and says, "Powder hand!" It's not a whole sentence, but anyone can tell she wants a little powder on her hand.

At this point in development, toddler brains have become so expert at language that toddlers begin to understand hundreds and hundreds of words. They learn to say new words nearly every day as their vocabulary blossoms and their ability to use more and more complex sentences improves. They also learn the rules that govern the language, including syntax, semantics, and pragmatics. For babies growing up with two languages, they accomplish all of this in two languages and often show skill in keeping the words from the two languages separate. They may know that mommy will respond if they say, "I want water," but when daddy is home, they need to say *agua* to get the same result. Of course, they make many mistakes—all children do at this stage—and that is all part of the learning process.

How does all this relate to dual language learners? Research shows that the process of learning how language works applies to all language learners (August and Shanahan, 2006). Whether you grow up in southern India, northern Sweden, or middle America, you have to learn that sounds connect together to become words that have meanings, that those words go together in a particular order, and that certain rules govern how they go together so you can understand others and they can understand you.

Generally, children who have a solid foundation in learning those rules will successfully transfer that knowledge to a new language. As an added advantage, a child who grows up bilingual is likely to have an easier time learning a third or fourth language or more. Experts also agree that children who grow up fully bilingual appear to have cognitive, social, and even financial advantages as they go through school and into their careers.

Experts tell us that during these first three years of development, the brain seems very successful at learning, coding, and making sense of two languages. There is some debate regarding whether learning in two languages may slow some toddlers down a bit at this stage, because they have more words to process and a more complex system to untangle, with two sets of grammar and vocabulary. There does not appear to be any lasting delay or confusion caused by learning in two languages, so this should not concern parents or caregivers. Overall, children who grow up with rich, engaging language supports in their two languages will experience cognitive advantages.

> *Experts tell us that during these first three years of development, the brain seems very successful at learning, coding, and making sense of two languages.*

It is important to take a look at how vocabulary is measured, too. Studies have shown that measuring vocabulary in only one language gives a deceptively low estimate of a young bilingual child's progress (Paradis, Genesee, and Crago, 2010). We often find that a child who may only know the colors *blue* and *yellow* in English might also know the colors *rojo y verde* (red and green) in Spanish. An assessment in one language will reveal only two colors, but in reality the child knows four. This leads to the belief that we underestimate early vocabulary knowledge of bilingual children, and any slowing in the first three years seems to be quickly overcome.

To grow up fully bilingual, infants and toddlers need high-quality language input in both languages. This entire process of language development must be supported in both (or all) of their languages. There are some additional considerations for children who begin the process of language development with only one language and start being exposed to a new language after they have mastered some of the components of language in their first language. Later in this book, you will find several sections that provide detailed guidance on how to work effectively with families and the community to make sure all your bilingual children get everything they need.

Simultaneous or Sequential Bilinguals

When children grow up with two or more languages right from the start, they are called *simultaneous bilinguals*. Children who start learning one language and then have a second language added after the age of two are called *sequential bilinguals*. Many experts believe these two types of bilingual children develop their languages differently. Timing is important, but we do not yet know exactly where the dividing line is when determining which category fits a particular child. This distinction may be more useful when children have passed the infant/toddler phase of development. If you care for a toddler who has made a lot of progress in her first language and comes to your program knowing none of your language, you might consider that child a sequential bilingual and provide supports accordingly.

Simultaneous bilingual children have two languages. Sequential bilinguals have a first language and a second language. Any sequentially bilingual child is likely to be stronger in one language than the other. The stronger, or more dominant, language may be the first one, but not always. In the case of simultaneous bilingual children, other factors may determine which language is dominant for that child, such as the child's relationship with the speakers of each language and the amount of time they spend interacting with others in that language.

In his observation notes about 20-month-old Luis, Mr. Pablo writes "Come on jugar" as an example of the toddler's attempts to communicate by combining words he knows from two languages. Mr. Pablo does not mark this as a source of concern, because it shows Luis can put together three words that communicate an invitation for his friend to join in his play. In fact, experts tell us that mixing words from two or more languages is a natural part of bilingual development and shows the brain's ability to use two languages as an asset (Espinosa, 2009). Some call it code-switching *or* code-mixing.

Barbara Zurer Pearson (2008) interpreted some studies that looked at how much input a child needs in each language to maintain a balanced bilingualism. Researchers have found that a child can learn to understand words in another language if she hears it as little as 20 percent of her waking hours. At that low rate of exposure, however, she likely will not be confident enough to create and produce her own sentences. Children—and adults—who understand a language but do not speak it are considered passive bilinguals. To progress in a language, a child needs to get far enough to actually say words in the language and invite interaction that will get her the feedback necessary to build her usage. If a child learns just enough to understand the language, the two-way interaction that the brain needs to build language will not occur.

On the other hand, we know that young children become fluent in a second language when they are exposed to it during about half of their waking hours. With language development, it is not always true that some is good but more is better. We need to break the old myth that young children need complete immersion in a new language to learn it well. The truth is nearly the opposite! Research has shown clearly that young children do best when they continue learning in their first language for part of every day while also spending part of the day learning in their new language. Studies of dual-language immersion programs have shown that children can maintain fluency in their home language and do well in their second language if the program offers about 50 percent of each. Spending more than 50 percent of the day with the new language does not seem to result in any more fluency or progress for young children. Other studies confirm that the minority language needs 40–60 percent exposure per day to grow it.

As with all other aspects of language development, this depends on the child's own interests, temperament, motivation, basic intelligence, and relationship with the person speaking the language. Think about what will happen when an infant or toddler goes to care where she hears the new, majority language in songs, fingerplays, stories, and high-quality interactions with rich interesting vocabulary, but then she goes home and hears her home language—the minority language—used to say, "Eat some more," or "Lie still so I can change you," or "Time for bed," and not much else.

But we can't just say to parents, "You should read to your baby." It's not always easy to read to a preverbal, squirmy baby or an active toddler. Because the child doesn't seem to understand the story, the parents may think reading does not make sense or that they need to force the child to pay attention to the book. It is very important for us to model or show videos so parents can see how to share books with children. We need to let them know that reading is just a way to talk more to the baby and to help her learn and build her brain. It is okay if they talk about the book or magazine pictures or what is going on outside the window—whatever they like to do with the baby. In later chapters of this book, we will share a number of strategies for helping parents provide high-quality, engaging language at home so the family's language can continue to thrive.

> *Research has shown clearly that young children do best when they continue learning in their first language for part of every day while also spending part of the day learning in their new language.*

Attitude is important for all the children and staff in your program. Babies can be so perceptive: They will notice if you treat some children differently from others or some languages differently from others. So, the issue of attitude is not just about your direct interactions with a particular child; it is about how you interact and model acceptance and love for all children and all their languages and cultures. That is how you create a positive atmosphere for everyone in your program.

Keep in mind an image of two icebergs that merge under water: Above the water and visible to the outside world, the child seems to be developing two peaks of language; however, under the surface, the brain makes sense of language as one unified system that gets expressed in different ways at different times. We believe that within the brain there is one system or structure that understands what language is and how it works—and it uses language input to increase and refine its ability to process and produce language. Some of the concepts a baby learns may be stored separately in one language or the other, but the brain has a basic understanding of how to use words to store concepts.

Whether a child is learning in one language or two or even more—the biological, social, neurological, and cognitive foundations of language stay the same. The brain does not learn words in isolation. Language is all about connections: the connections between sounds, the connections between meanings, and the connections between people. We know that brain development in the early years depends on strong relationships with nurturing caregivers who really know the baby and respond to her signals and attempts at communication. When this relationship is hampered because the baby and caregiver do not understand each other, a great communication gap can occur. We will look at ways to enable all caregivers to connect with infants in all of their languages. This is so important, both for meeting the child's immediate need to communicate and for developing a long-term bond that will be strengthened by that language connection.

REFLECTION QUESTIONS

- What are two things that second-language development has in common with the development of the first language?

- What is the most important message you think parents need to understand about how their child is learning in two languages?

CHAPTER 5

Supporting Development in Two or More Languages

What can caregivers do to effectively support home- and second-language development in infants and toddlers?

FOCUS QUESTIONS

- What are the different reasons why an infant or toddler might be growing up with two languages?

- Why do we need language—what do we use it for?

After you think about your answers to these questions, try asking other people to share their thoughts on the topic. For example, try bringing the second question to your next playgroup or staff meeting or luncheon and see what kinds of responses you hear.

When you really take some time to answer this question and discuss it with your peers, the list of responses can vary widely. Here are some of the answers that may come up:

- To express our emotions
- To express our thoughts
- To get attention
- To get our needs met
- To understand what other people are communicating
- To learn new information
- To share our passions
- To catalog information

- To play and enjoy
- To understand how other people feel and react to us
- To participate
- To be part of things
- To inform someone of something they don't seem to know
- To make things happen

Keeping all of these different uses for language in mind helps teachers and caregivers think about and plan effective strategies that go far beyond basic vocabulary building.

The strategies described in this chapter can be applied in the home language or in the second language. They are all developmentally appropriate language-building techniques. You may do more in one language or the other, but all children should have these experiences in their home language at least part of every day.

Narrating the Action

Talk about what you are doing, talk about what the baby is doing, refer to the baby by name often—especially when narrating play between two babies. Pay attention to language—repeat words, say things with a rhythm or a rhyme: "Let's clean up, give me that cup. Let's clean UP, give me the CUP!"

Sing a little song, such as, "It's changing time right now; it's changing time right now; let's change your diaper, it's changing time right now," maybe using the tune of "Farmer in the Dell." Or, repeat the same words every time you do the same thing, "When we go to the playground, we walk."

Building Relationships

Remember that the main purpose for language is communication, which develops through caring and responsive relationships. Raikes and Edwards (2009) said they could not stress enough how important the relationship is between caregiver and infants and toddlers. That relationship is a large concern for babies in out-of-home care.

Yes, children will need language later on to succeed in school, but that is not what the infant brain focuses on during the first two years, and it is not what we should focus on. The infant/toddler caregiver's focus should be on helping babies communicate what is on their minds, helping them understand what is on others' minds, and helping them interact with each other. This natural approach is the most effective way to help all young children develop language. The connections between children and adults and between children and their peers create the responsive settings the brain needs to make language progress. When caring for young children who come from different language backgrounds, we must pay attention to connecting with each one as an individual so we can learn how to reach them effectively.

In their book *Extending the Dance in Infant and Toddler Caregiving* (2009), Helen Raikes and Carolyn Pope Edwards share features of healthy caregiver-child relationships. Some of these can be especially helpful in our work with children from different language and cultural backgrounds.

- The teacher and child seek eye contact with one another.
- The teacher and child brighten at the sight of one another.
- The teacher and child adjust their responses to each other.
- The child relaxes when held by the teacher.
- The child and teacher seek physical contact with one another.

These social-emotional components of communication can be even more important as caregivers strive to build relationships with children and families who speak other languages.

Miss Linda is the primary caregiver for three infants in her classroom: Nine-month-old Akbar has Arabic parents who speak very little English; 10-month-old Cho Hee lives with her Korean mom and grandparents; and 11-month-old Marisol seems to respond only to Spanish. Miss Linda sits on the floor with her babies around her and sings a little song with hand gestures. She sings only in English, but encourages the babies to vocalize and clap their hands. Whatever sound one of the babies makes, Miss Linda looks that child in the eye and smiles and repeats the sound. The babies seem fascinated with Miss Linda and try to engage her again and again in making their sounds. Miss Linda makes a note of this on the parent report sheets to share at the end of the day.

Work hard to build a bond with each baby using genuine affection and intentional non-verbal communication. Try to support everything you say with actions to add meaning and help build mutual understanding. In this kind of atmosphere, you will often see older infants and toddlers adopting the good habit of showing you what they're saying even when they are talking to another toddler! When young children do not understand each other, it is hard to get along. Learning how to help their friends understand what they mean gives children the experience of success with their social skills.

Nonverbal Communication

Nonverbal communication includes all the different things we do to get our message across without words. In infant/toddler groups, we use these supports in addition to spoken words. We do not replace oral language; we enhance it. Some nonverbal methods that work well with infants and toddlers include the following suggestions.

- **Joint focus**—also called *shared reference*—means making sure you and the child are paying attention to the same thing when you are talking. You can either take a second to follow the child's gaze and talk about what he is interested in, or you can draw the child's attention to the topic you want to mention. But you should not start talking about the ants on the ground while the baby is looking up at the clouds in the sky.

- **Pointing** seems simple, but it actually contributes powerfully to language development, which makes it even more important in a multilingual group. Pointing allows you to direct the child's attention to whatever you are talking about, and it allows the child to show clearly when he understands what you are saying. That is why we depend on pointing to help us in formal and informal language assessments. When a child comes to you for the first time, spend some time helping him understand how pointing works and how you can use it together to bridge the communication gap.

- **Gestures** draw attention to key words when you talk to another person. Luckily (well, it's probably more purposeful than lucky), infants and toddlers are very adept at using your gestures to help them make sense of your words. Also, they quickly adopt gesture communication even before they can speak. Think of the infants younger than a year old who wave bye-bye or hold their arms up when they want you to hold them. We know gestures are effective for both adult and child communicators—so they can certainly add to your effectiveness as you talk to young dual language learners.

- **Facial expressions** should be exaggerated but only to make sure the babies clearly understand your meaning—not so much so that you start looking like a scary clown or a bad actor! Just use your natural tendency to support your verbal communications with facial expressions. With children from different language backgrounds, you need to make the extra effort to stop and face them so they can reliably see your expressions. Also take the time to study the baby's face when he tries to communicate with you, so you can get a better understanding of his message.

- **Demonstrating** is a great language builder and a great bridge. Why just say, "Jump!" when you can actually jump? It is always interesting to see how infants and toddlers respond to demonstrating an action. Because of their different levels of neurological development and physical coordination, they may imitate your actions very well or they may do something that seems unrelated. They may even act as if they have no idea what you are trying to do (which is always funny, such as when a teacher is trying to show a child how to jump and bounces all around while the toddler just stands there staring at her). Remember, though, the child's physical ability to copy your action does not necessarily indicate how well your demonstration helps him understand the message. Even if the children don't move with you, they likely have better comprehension. Some infants and toddlers respond well to having the adult actually move their hands or bodies into place to do the action. Be cautious about using this hands-on approach until you are sure the child will tolerate it, and keep it a positive experience.

- **Tone of voice** also adds meaning to our words. Infants actually learn to use tone of voice or inflection well before they speak their first word, so it is an aspect of communication for which the brain is very well prepared. Be mindful of your tone, because it may be the most noticeable part of your speech for young dual language learners. Even if your words are positive, a loud voice can give a negative impression to those who don't understand the words you use.

- **Props** can be anything you use to add to your meaning. Teachers are accustomed to using props during story times or songs, but there are many other times when props can be helpful as well. Think about using props when explaining classroom rules to children. You could just say the rule, but what if you showed the children two dolls running and one fell down? Props can also be models—like the snake, ball, and pancake you make out of playdough to demonstrate shapes, or a bridge you make in the block area to illustrate that they can build in ways other than straight up.

- **Pictures** can be very helpful in providing clues to meaning. Catalog cutouts taped to the toy shelves help all children see where each item gets put away, regardless of language skills. Borrow from a well-known special education strategy, and create a picture communication board so toddlers can show you what they want by pointing to the picture for the bathroom or the picture of a cup of juice.

- **Books**, especially familiar ones, can be a great source of communication pictures because you and the children already know the pictures and what they mean in the context of the story. When talking to dual language learners in the soft-toy area, you can pick up a book and help them make the connection, "You are hugging the bear. Here are the three bears in our story today!" Ideally, you could stock up on books with two languages. Then you can pick up the same book in the child's home language and say, "Tu eres abrazando el oso."

- **Sign language** is currently a phenomenal trend in the early childhood world, and thousands of families and teachers of hearing children, both in the United States and in many other countries, use it. Unlike other trends that have come and gone, baby sign language seems to be here to stay, because it helps infants and toddlers build communication and learn language.

American Sign Language (ASL) is a true language and can be a great addition to a teacher's repertoire. Some teachers start with basic survival words or illustrative words to enhance classroom communication, and there are many websites, books, and videos to help, such as sign2me.com or babysigns .com. Other teachers may choose to develop ASL fluency by taking a class at a local community college. (Just remember, ASL has its own sentence structure, so true ASL does not just replace English words with signs.) Many ASL signs for the beginning words used in preschool really look like what they represent, so they can help you show your non-English-speaking children what you are talking about. For example, the sign for *ball* looks like you are literally holding a ball in your hands. You can use that sign to ask a DLL to bring you the ball or to play with the ball. Always use signs along with spoken words. The goal is to build and enhance oral language, not to replace it.

If all of the staff in a school or program use basic ASL signs, the children will see the same signs consistently, no matter who is talking to them. Knowing a little ASL will also prove helpful if you have a child with hearing loss in your classroom. Many therapists in the United States use ASL in early intervention programs to assist children with language delays, even if their home language is English. When those children arrive in preschool, their experience can be so much better if they find a class full of friends and teachers who know what they are saying with their signs.

ASL can help children from different language backgrounds play together. The clear, visual nature of signing makes it a natural tool to help friends overcome language barriers. More experienced children can help welcome new peers to the classroom, because ASL signs make it easy for one child to teach words to another child.

Infant/toddler teachers who use ASL in their classrooms report a quieter, calmer environment, because children from different language backgrounds and abilities all have a way to communicate and to get their needs met. With a room full of children and a room full of different languages, ASL can bring everyone together with shared understanding.

Music and Movement

Singing and dancing are part of nearly every culture. Bring in music that families listen to at home, as well as your favorites, to involve everyone from the smallest infant to the most active toddler in the joy of moving to music. The patterns, rhythms, and repetition in songs are strong components of language learning and can help children develop their home language and their new language together.

Music is wonderful, but having it on in the background all day may actually inhibit language development—especially for your dual language learners. To accomplish the work of listening and making sense out of speech sounds, as well as figuring out how those speech sounds work differently in two languages, children need to hear plenty of clear language input from responsive adults and peers. So consider these two points:

- A lot of sound in the background can mask the sounds of speech you use with the children. They may have difficulty perceiving the subtle differences between certain sounds and may have a hard time focusing on your language over the music.

- When the environment is quiet, adults are more likely to fill the silence by talking, singing, and interacting. If you observe classrooms where music plays in the background at all times, you may see long gaps when the adults do not say anything. With the background music going, they may not even realize it. This does not imply that every teacher needs to talk every minute of the day, but the amount of talking may fall below acceptable levels in the presence of constant background noise.

Learn Key Words in Each Child's Language

When a family enrolls in your program, make sure you find out the language(s) spoken at home, so you can learn a few key words to use when the child first comes to you for care. One of the most important key words is the child's name! It is essential to make this effort. Some names are easier to pronounce than others, but every child's name is part of his or her identity and deserves correct pronunciation.

Make a list of words that you think will make the child feel welcomed, warm, safe, comfortable, and loved from his first day. Ask the parents to help you learn to say these words in the child's home language. Some programs send a list and a small digital recorder home so the parents can record the words and the teacher can learn by listening. This also gives the parents the chance to teach you familiar words rather than dictionary words. For example, a two-year-old child might only know his grandmother as "Nannie." He has no idea what you mean if you say, "Your grandma will be here soon."

Activity: Easy Weave

Children discover that tape and glue are not the only ways to hold things together. A three-dimensional way to hold things together is to wrap, tie, and weave materials together.

Dual Language Adaptation: Look for activities such as this one that can be learned once and practiced in lots of different ways. Learn some of the key words for this activity in the home languages of the children, and take the time to identify each item you will use before getting started. Once the children have learned to do this activity with your home-language coaching, bring weaving activities out at other times. Gradually, as they get familiar with the activity of weaving, switch to introducing the weaving activity by speaking only in English. Once they understand the concept in their home language, you can build on that knowledge by helping them learn the English words for the same activities.

(An adaptation of an activity from *First Art for Toddlers and Twos* by MaryAnn F. Kohl)

Print and Labels

We like to see environmental print in early childhood classrooms, even though the infants and toddlers will not actually read it. Still, it is a good idea to post labels around the room in the languages of the children for adults to read. Be thoughtful when doing this; you do not need to clutter everything with unnecessary stickers. A few labels in the kitchen area will remind you of some vocabulary in the languages of the children to use while they are playing there. A label over the sink might say, "Wash your hands," in each language you need, complete with pronunciation cues.

No Drive-By Talking

If you change a baby with your back to the room, and you think you can fill the language environment of the other babies at the same time—think again. Infants do not recognize their names as a sign to focus on your words, so they hear lots of words floating around but don't know what to connect them to. Each baby in your care should have a good share of your time with direct interaction and play. "Drive-by talking" happens when caregivers talk while moving around the room and don't really focus on what the baby is focusing on. The caregiver may say, "Oh, that's a bird; do you hear the bird?" but the baby is completely absorbed in trying to grab his foot. Or the caregiver may be talking and not even realize that the baby is vocalizing and looking for feedback. One of the saddest sights to observe in a child care room is when an infant coos or babbles and then waits, but no adults respond because they are all too busy elsewhere. When children are trying to make sense out of two languages and learn concepts and meaning in both of their languages, we need to try harder to provide comprehensible input—input that connects to each child and to his immediate focus of attention.

Talking about Books

Literacy expert Betty Bardige (2008) really emphasizes this interpretation of the famous Hart and Risley study: She reminds us that it is not just about the number of words a baby hears; it is about the kind of words. Her focus is on play language. Think about how much richer, more interesting, and more easily remembered is language you exchange during fun play activities or when you look at a book together, compared to language you use to manage behavior or language in a structured lesson.

Language Opportunities Throughout the Day

A great way to add authentic language experiences to the day for infants and toddlers is to think about all the areas of the room and all of the activities of each day. Much of the formal and informal infant/toddler curriculum revolves around care routines—and these are perfect opportunities to work on language skills. If you have ever used the *Infant/Toddler Environment Rating Scale* (ITERS) by Harms, Cryer, and Clifford (2006), you can see evidence of this premise throughout the scale. The ITERS rates the effectiveness of infant/toddler classrooms. Some observation items specifically refer to language, but when you take a closer look, you will see that high scores depend on some use of language in more than half of the scoring items. For example, item 5 is about "displays for children," but in addition to visual displays, this item looks for evidence that "staff talk to the children about displayed materials." You might think that item 7 on "meals and snacks" is about nutrition, but to get a good score, observers need to see "staff talk with children and provide a pleasant time."

These examples show just a few of the situations where conversations with young children matter. With dual language learners, you will want to build home language into those conversations as much as you can—aim for a 50/50 split if you have bilingual staff. If you are not bilingual, you should still emphasize rich, engaging talk in the different areas of the room, but put greater focus on your nonverbal strategies to make sure dual language learners understand.

The Importance of Silliness

Everyone has their own comfort level with silliness. It can be a wonderful way to capture children's attention and help them get absorbed in fun and engaging language.

- Silly voices help children identify different characters in a story.

- Silly interactions help us bond with children in a fun and joyful way.

- Silly times make up some of the most memorable moments for us and for children.

- Silliness supports children's imagination and creativity.

- Laughter is good for our health—and our quality of life!

The value of all these strategies comes in using them to help children from different languages understand your language and to help them understand you when you try to pronounce their languages, too. An added benefit of developing these habits is that you also model these effective strategies for the parents and the children at the same time, so all communication at home and in your program can improve.

The language needs of each child will differ, and you will have to get to know each one as an individual with his own characteristics and experiences. For a child who comes with little or no experience in your language, you should use as much of his language as possible in the beginning. You can then begin transitioning to your language. You can support another child who already knows both languages with a smaller proportion of home language during the day.

Always keep in mind that communication is the most important goal. If you are working with a child in English, but he has something he really wants to ask or tell you in his first language, go ahead and respond in the home language if you can. The information can later be transferred to English when he is ready, but the benefit to your relationship with that child is immediate.

REFLECTION QUESTIONS

- What are some strategies in this chapter that you knew already? Can you see ways in which your current practices can be effective with infants and toddlers who are growing up bilingual?

- List three strategies from this chapter that you could use as the topic for a parent-education event. Why do think your choices are important for parents?

CHAPTER 5 PLANNING FORM

Supporting Multiple Languages

Strategy	Child 1 Home language:	Child 2 Home language:	Child 3 Home language:	Child 4 Home language:

Planning Form

Use the planning form on page 109 to list strategies from this chapter that you plan to use in your work with infants and toddlers, then note your comments to adjust your strategies for each child.

6 Welcoming Diverse Families and Encouraging Them to Enroll

How can we attract and enroll diverse families?

FOCUS QUESTIONS

- Where can you learn what languages are prevalent in your community?

- Is it enough to have a list of the local languages? What additional information would help you attract more diverse families?

Welcoming diverse families should start from the outside in. What do your advertisements look like? What's on your website? Are your signs and brochures in different languages? Do they show different faces? Some reports have talked about the lower percentage of children from immigrant families enrolling their children in child care programs. Yet, diverse child care programs have so much to offer families from different countries. Your program may be the first service the family connects with. At this starting point, you can help the family have a positive experience in the American style of family involvement, and you can help them connect with any other services the family may need to survive and thrive. So, not only is it good business to attract diverse families, it is also a great community service.

Strategies

This "Top 10" list of strategies will help increase the effectiveness of your community outreach.

10 Make it clear that your program welcomes diversity by posting greetings in the languages of your community on signs, ads, and your website.

9 Include images of racial and ethnic diversity in the pictures, art, and graphics you use to represent your program.

8 Employ staff members who speak more than one language at your front desk, in classrooms, and throughout your program.

7 Provide staff training to enhance cultural awareness and sensitivity.

6 Teach staff members to greet new families with sensitivity to language differences. Speak slowly, speak clearly, avoid slang, be patient, check for understanding, use gestures, and write things down. Make a picture communication book so families who don't speak the language can show you what they need.

5 Take a tour of your classrooms to make sure they are well stocked with culturally and linguistically authentic displays and materials. Never assume. Just because families have a Hispanic last name does not mean they speak Spanish, nor does it mean the child grew up around people wearing sombreros and serapes. To be culturally appropriate, materials need to match the child's experiences.

4 After a family has enrolled their child, take the time to learn enough about their specific language and cultural background so you can prepare to teach their child and meet their needs.

3 Ask families which language they prefer for receiving communications from your program, *and* ask them if they prefer written notices, emails, texts, or phone calls.

2 Rewrite your parent handbook and enrollment papers to use fewer words and simpler language, and incorporate pictures, graphics, and icons to increase readability.

1 Make the extra effort to learn and pronounce the parents' and child's names correctly so you can begin your relationship with true respect!

The Singh family was looking for the best child care setting for their first son, aged six months. They were part of a diverse community, yet time after time they would visit child care homes and centers that only had pictures of white children and families on their English-only brochures, posters, and displays. The Singhs felt somewhat uncomfortable in each of those places. As they were getting to the bottom of their list, they visited the Sunshine Day Care Center. There was a welcome sign as they drove into the parking lot—in four languages! As soon as they entered the building, they could see displays showing diverse families and children. The receptionist greeted them and asked them if they would like information in English or in another language. And that is where they placed their son.

REFLECTION QUESTIONS

- To gain truly diverse perspectives as you evaluate the materials used by your program, whom could you enlist to help you do that evaluation and give some different points of view?

- Have you ever been in a situation where you felt like an outsider? How can recalling that feeling help you and your staff think of better ways to reach out and make new families feel welcome?

Planning Form

Use the planning form on page 110 to list the strategies from this chapter that apply to your program. Then check off the ones you have accomplished, and list the languages used for each strategy. Your goals will be to address additional languages in your community and the unchecked strategies.

Engaging Families to Participate

How can we get diverse families to take an active role in their babies' care?

FOCUS QUESTIONS

- Can you think of a family who just doesn't seem to get involved in the activities of your program? What do you wish you knew to turn that situation around?

- What are the factors in an immigrant family's life that might inhibit them from participating as much as you would like?

We have talked about ways to attract diverse families to enroll in your program. The next step is to encourage each family to get truly involved as your partner in caring for and educating their young child. When families speak little English or come from a culture with a strong separation between families and programs, they may not respond to casual invitations to join in. You will need to get to know each family and to build a relationship with them on their own terms. All enrollment paperwork should be followed up by an in-person meeting or home visit to get beyond the impersonal paperwork and get to know the real answers you need.

The first contact you have with a family after their child enrolls must be about something happy and positive. You cannot build a positive relationship if the first call from you is about their child biting someone or showing possible developmental delays. Every caregiver involved with their child should make an effort to contact the family in the first week and share with them some nice things that show their child is thriving in your care. We know that toddlers cannot talk well enough to give an accurate report, but when you do not speak the same language as the family, you cannot give an effective verbal report either. Think about how much better that worried mom will feel if you can show her a couple of photos of her smiling toddler playing happily with toys during the day. These kinds of positive interactions lead to a stronger bond with the families.

When Ana was enrolled in the Our World Child Care Center, her mom received a call from one of the other parents. In Spanish, the language they share, the other mom welcomed Ana's mom to the program and told her some of the fun activities her child enjoyed there. She asked Ana's mom if she had any questions about the program and promised to stay in touch by phone or email. The next day, Ana's mom realized she did not understand what the teacher was saying—something about a parent meeting. She called her new friend and got the information she needed to attend the first parents' event of the year at her daughter's new center.

Have a variety of options so family members can participate and help in your program. You could invite them to come in and read to the children in their home language—which would be great, but not everyone is comfortable reading aloud in front of a group of squirmy toddlers. What other opportunities can you offer that would incorporate their language and culture?

- "Play buddies" come in and play with the children using their home language.

- Outdoor walkers can help take the children outside and provide conversations in their home language.

- Singers can share traditional songs and nursery rhymes.

- Rockers and snugglers (that is a language all its own!) come in to rock and snuggle any child who needs it.

- Office help—for people who are not comfortable working directly with children, you can help them get to know your program and staff by asking them to help in your office.

- Document readers can read letters and policy statements after you have them translated to make sure they are appropriate for your audience.

- Environmental helpers can pitch in by washing toys, mending curtains, or painting equipment.

- Crafters can create decorations and toys for your environment.

Another approach to getting parents involved in your program is to provide services and activities that will help them. Take parents to the public library; let them know it is a great place for parents, even if they only have babies and even if they speak another language. After all, it is critical to help parents understand that if we do not speak their child's home language while he is in care, then the parents must do more to build literacy and language fluency in the home language at home. You might offer ESL classes or computer classes for parents at your center, or hold family potluck dinners so they can take a night off from cooking and meet other families.

Be sure to begin your relationship with parents as a partnership. Get to know what strengths they bring to the partnership. How do they talk to their baby or share books with their baby? As you continue to build positive relationships with the parents, consider these suggestions based on *Extending the Dance in Infant and Toddler Caregiving* (2009) by Helen H. Raikes and Carolyn Pope Edwards:

- Get to know the parents on a variety of different levels.

- Notice the positive moments between the parent and child.

- Support the parents as the experts on their own child by noticing and using the same words they use to describe their child.

- Take the time to listen to the positive stories the parent wants to share.

Share what you have to offer to parents from a position of collaboration. Help parents learn how to talk to their babies and read to them and sing to them. Talk about what is happening throughout the day and ask questions. Simply sending books home with families is sometimes not enough to change their home literacy behaviors. Offer activity workshops at different days and times—and by all means, serve food at every gathering!

You may notice that parents need help with parenting skills, but offering a workshop that implies they are not good parents is not the best approach. Try offering a "Super Science" workshop for families to attend together, or a multicultural cooking class. These hands-on topics attract a lot of families and can effectively model good strategies for exploring and talking with children.

One significant challenge that many infant/toddler programs face is how to help parents understand that giving up their home language is likely to result in problems for the child and for the family. Parents often desire to have their child experience only English while in care. Following is some information you can use as you explain that you share the parents' goal to have their child learn and succeed in English, but that support for their home language is the best way to get there.

Children need time to continue strengthening the learning they have already done in their first language, even while they learn the second. The brain does not have a problem growing up with two or more languages at the same time. Problems seem to occur when a new language overtakes the first and somehow interferes with language and content learning. The studies summarized by the National Literacy Panel (August and Shanahan, 2006) reveal no short-term or long-term advantages to total English immersion in preschool. Children who learn literacy skills first in their home language are likely to transfer those skills successfully to English (Paez and Rinaldi, 2006). Other researchers, such as Collier (1987), have made the case that it takes six years or more for children to achieve sufficient academic fluency in a new language to succeed in school. Clearly, preschoolers need more time to continue learning and experiencing the world in their home language if that is true. One drawback of too-quick immersion is that young children have to spend too much of their valuable early-learning time struggling with new vocabulary when they could focus on actively learning concepts.

> *The brain does not have a problem growing up with two or more languages at the same time.*

All children need to feel equally respected and loved. The home language is an integral part of each child's identity. Children's self-esteem will suffer if they attend a preschool that makes their language seem less worthy than English. A study by Chang et al. (2007) found that Spanish-speaking children who did not receive support in their home language in preschool were more likely to be socially isolated, victims of bullying, and viewed negatively by teachers. Children who do not receive support in their home language likely will lose their expressive ability in that first language, which is critical to their bonds with their families (Wong Fillmore, 1991).

Children need adults who can form loving, nurturing relationships with them to help their brains develop to their full potential. This means they need to continue the strong bonds and the communication with their parents, and this requires continued growth in their home language. It also means they need teachers who speak their language, so they can gain the full benefits of the human connectedness that makes the best learning possible in those crucial early years.

Of course, educators need to understand and respect parental values. It is not respectful, however, to go along with a parent's wishes if you know there is a better way and there is research to back it up. Teachers and administrators need to make it clear that their language policy includes plans for each child to spend some time each day learning in the home language. Parents need to know that they should read to their child in their home language and talk about the books they read. They should share family stories, inside jokes, songs, rhymes, confidences, and expressions of affection.

Teachers and families can work as partners to share knowledge about the language and about the individual needs and progress of each child. "By supporting the home language of each child while scaffolding their English learning, educators (and society) have much to gain and nothing to lose. Being bilingual is surely an asset in today's world" (Nemeth, 2009).

REFLECTION QUESTIONS

- What do other schools and programs in your area do to encourage parent engagement? Can you establish partnerships or informal sharing to get new ideas?

- How has technology changed the way you can connect with parents and keep them interested in participating?

Planning Form

Use the planning form on page 111 to list the tasks that parents can do in or for your program and the roles they can play.

Culturally and Linguistically Appropriate Environments

What should we see in diverse infant/toddler environments?

FOCUS QUESTIONS

- What do you think about when choosing decorations and learning materials for your environment? Do the images and items reflect the cultures and languages of your area?

- What would you like to learn more about to feel confident in making your environment more culturally and linguistically appropriate?

The environment has a powerful influence on how young children learn, how teachers teach, and how parents participate. With some mindful planning, any infant/toddler environment can be culturally and linguistically appropriate. The most important points you will want to address include the following:

Display posters, three-dimensional displays and artwork, and environmental print that match the languages and cultures of the families. Make sure the environment is pleasing for the parents as well as the babies. Parents need to feel respected and connected to feel comfortable leaving their baby with you. The first step in setting up a proper environment is learning what languages families speak and a little about their cultures. Even if you know a family's language, you may make missteps in preparing the environment if you do not know more about them. For example, not all Thai families are the same: some come from the city and will recognize urban references throughout your classroom, but others are from the mountains, and they may feel uncomfortable in the presence of too many pictures of city buildings, traffic, and restaurants. Be sure that the images you use are respectful and individualized, rather than cartoonish and silly.

> **Note:** See the website of the U.S. Copyright Office for an explanation of fair use within an educational context. http://www .copyright.gov/fls/ fl102.html

Miss Ingrid learned she would have a new child in her classroom on Monday and the family had recently moved to the area from Vietnam. As she looked around her room, she realized she had no images that reflected the Vietnamese culture or people, but she did not know where to find posters on such short notice. She took a couple of Vietnamese storybooks from her library shelf and brought them to the copy store to have color copies made of some of the pages, and she had those posted to decorate the room by Monday morning.

Place language reminder cards; functional labels; children's and adult books; access to iPod, iPad, Internet, or other technologies; and music in the needed languages throughout your space to make the caregiver's job easier. Use the environment not only to support the families and children but also to make things easier for caregivers. The easier it is to pick up bilingual books with the pronunciations written in, the more likely it is that the caregiver will use them to learn and practice new words to use with the children.

The real items and items that directly relate to each child's home environment should outnumber the items you order from catalogs. Search for authentic items that represent each child's language, culture, and home life. This can be a great way to encourage parent participation. Ask parents to bring in clean, empty food containers the child will recognize, as well as recordings of music they sing and listen to at home. A CD of songs in Spanish is nice, but it may not be the real children's songs and rhymes used by the family at home. Use digital cameras to take pictures of buildings and sights in your neighborhood, and add those to the block area, or make puzzles, games, and class-made books the children can really relate to.

Save the recorded songs and stories for caregivers, to help them learn the languages! A "listening center" is not advisable for infant/toddler classrooms. Many catalogs sell machines and headphones for this purpose, but remember that the Kuhl (2010) research showed infants and toddlers learn little or no language via recordings.

There should be books in all the languages you expect to encounter.
This is a must. Some languages are hard to find, so you might enhance the English books you have by getting key words translated and putting those words on stickers that you can add to your favorite books. There should be at least 10 books per child and per language. For example, if you have seven children in your class and three have a home language other than English, you would need 70 books (10 per child), plus another 30 (10 for each home language), for a total of 100 books.

Choose puppets and props that you will really put to use. Puppets and props bring stories to life for children who are learning a language. Too often, classrooms have a lovely puppet display gathering dust and never used. Puppets are a wonderful way to add character and fun to practicing language. They may help a shy child feel comfortable or help a distracted child focus on language.

A great language reminder for caregivers would be rings of index cards that could be placed in different areas of the classroom. Ask parents or volunteers to help you spell out key words phonetically, so you can say them to the children in their home languages while they are engaged in related activities. The index cards might have words such as *red, green, brush, paper,* and *smock* in the art area; or *diaper, wipe, wet, clean, messy, bottom, pants,* and *legs* in the changing area.

Make the effort to collect realistic dress-up clothes for dramatic play. Fake costumes will not reflect the cultures of your children. Not all Hispanic children identify with sombreros! Again, families can help with this collection.

Catalogs can be a great source for multiethnic dolls, pretend food, and utensils that can create first and lasting impressions in your environment. Simple puzzles and other toys representing different people and environments are becoming more available. Keep looking for the newest catalogs to find things that were previously impossible to obtain.

Consider using digital recorders and digital cameras when caring for diverse infants and toddlers. A recorder allows you to record a child's sounds and her early attempts at language so you can get help translating. This enables you to respond accurately and to support the home-language development while also supporting progress in English. Some digital cameras have a voice-recording feature. But even without that feature, digital cameras have many uses in early childhood programs. Take pictures of the children, their families, and their activities, and use them to create books, posters, puzzles, games, and displays. Cameras also allow you to take pictures that can help you show the parents how happy their thriving baby is while in your care.

Replace many of your collections of unrecognizable plastic manipulatives with collections of things that children know about from home. They can learn to count and sort with socks or match sizes with large and small cupcake cups and pans. This helps children build on prior knowledge to learn concepts because they are not distracted by having to figure out what the plastic things are and what they are called.

The goal of any environment for linguistically and culturally diverse infants and toddlers is to meet the needs of the families and the caregivers as well as the children. By using as many realistic and authentic items as possible, you can create a welcoming and responsive setting filled with language-rich activities that strongly connect learning in your program to experiences at home.

REFLECTION QUESTIONS

- Now that you have read this chapter and taken a closer look at your environment, what do you find that seems to work well to meet the cultural and linguistic needs of your children?

- What do you think will be the biggest change you need to make in your environment? Where can you find what you need for this change?

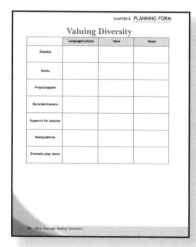

Planning Form

Take a look around your environment and use the form on page 112 to list the things that represent different languages and cultures and list the things you still need.

CHAPTER 9

Cultural Awareness and Responsiveness

What do we need to know and do to honor different cultures?

FOCUS QUESTIONS

- To begin building your cultural awareness, list five key parts of your own culture that you identify with. Think about how you learned these things.

- Whom do you know who shares these key practices and characteristics? Do those shared factors bring you together?

- Whom are you close to in your life who does NOT share those cultural factors with you?

- How are your relationships able to thrive with people who do some things differently than you do?

Culture is part of each of us, and each of us shares some elements with different cultures. Language is embedded in culture, so understanding language differences is enhanced by an awareness of cultural differences. In this chapter we emphasize awareness, sensitivity, and responsiveness to cultural differences. We do not, however, expect every reader to become a culture expert, because each person's experience within his or her cultural context is unique. Not everyone from your community believes the same things or eats the same things or values the same things. Culture helps us to understand other people, but it does not completely define them. What we should aim for is an attitude of openness to learning about others and accepting that their cultures may steer them in different directions than we might take at times.

> *Culture helps us to understand other people, but it does not completely define them.*

Mr. Jim was sitting with his feet up on a chair when a new family entered the room. He had taken his shoes off because they had given him a blister. He noticed that the parents seemed uncomfortable and would not look at him as he tried to talk to them. Later he learned that many Thai people consider it an insult to be shown the bottoms of your feet. Of course, Mr. Jim had no way of knowing that specific fact, but he knew he had to work harder to observe people's behavior to learn more about how people from different cultures react to different situations. He asked his director to schedule that topic for an upcoming professional-development day.

As an infant/toddler care professional, you cannot be expected to learn everything about every culture represented in your program. You can, however, try to get to know the individuals in your program—both the families and the children—and let them guide your cultural understanding. You can strive for more awareness of differences and similarities rather than making assumptions or generalizations. You can try to be more sensitive in your speech and actions to avoid giving offense, but accept that you might make a mistake and offend someone—just as someone might unknowingly offend you. An attitude of acceptance and tolerance will foster those all-important relationships. Use your awareness and sensitivity to enhance your knowledge of the dreams and needs of the adults and children with whom you work so that you can be responsive in your words and actions. The ITERS classroom rating scale captures this approach in item 24, *"Promoting acceptance of diversity*—cultural awareness shown in materials, interactions, and activities."

Now let's look at the guidance provided by national leaders on this topic.

Here are the 10 Head Start Multicultural Principles (Office of Head Start, 2010).

1. Every individual is rooted in culture.

2. The cultural groups represented in the communities and families of each Head Start program are the primary sources for culturally relevant programming.

3. Culturally relevant and diverse programming requires learning accurate information about the cultures of different groups and discarding stereotypes.

4. Addressing cultural relevance in making curriculum choices and adaptations is a necessary, developmentally appropriate practice.

5. Every individual has the right to maintain his or her own identity while acquiring the skills required to function in our diverse society.

6. Effective programs for children who speak languages other than English require continued development of the first language while the acquisition of English is facilitated.

7. Culturally relevant programming requires staff who both reflect and are responsive to the community and families served.

8. Multicultural programming for children enables children to develop an awareness of, respect for, and appreciation of individual cultural differences.

9. Culturally relevant and diverse programming examines and challenges institutional and personal biases.

10. Culturally relevant and diverse programming and practices are incorporated in all systems and services and are beneficial to all adults and children.

The National Association for the Education of Young Children (NAEYC) offers the position statement *Where we stand on responding to linguistic and cultural diversity*, which echoes the themes from the Head Start principles and adds a recommendation about language diversity, stating that programs should "help develop essential concepts in the child's first language and within cultural contexts that they understand."

These recommendations provide excellent general guideposts, but it still remains the responsibility of each caregiver to navigate cultural differences in his or her own work. Although you want to support each family's culture, this does not mean you have to go along with aspects of their culture that are against the law, the policy of the program, or your personal ethics. The challenge lies in developing a level of self-awareness so you can discern the times when a different way of doing things could be okay and the times when you cannot compromise. This challenge can prove very tricky in infant/toddler care because the activities of the professional caregiver resemble the activities of the parents, and finding common ground on how those activities should be carried out is not always easy. These decisions have to be made on a case-by-case basis within each organization.

You might think it is fine for children to use pacifiers well into their third year, but your co-teacher may think that is disgusting. Is this difference based in your cultures, personal opinions, or differences between practices in your own families, or is it a topic that you each learned about in different professional-development events? Cultural differences do not always explain different approaches. People may believe they engage in some practice with their children because it is part of their culture, but another person from the same culture might disagree. The best and most useful way to find the answer to these dilemmas comes, once again, through relationships. Defining cultural practices often matters less than getting to know each individual child and family and what matters to them—regardless of whether or not it comes from culture.

When planning conversations with parents and staff, you might explore the following topics that are often affected by cultural beliefs and practices:

- Self-help skills
- Infant/toddler schedules
- Issues around feeding and food choices
- Music and dancing
- Book reading and storytelling
- Ways to talk to infants and toddlers

- Discipline
- Demands vs. indulgence
- Comforting methods
- Celebrations and holidays
- Male and female roles
- Appropriate play choices
- Treatment of minor illnesses

Here are some resources that will help you develop policies and approaches that can work for your program.

Derman-Sparks, L., and Edwards, J. O. 2010. *Anti-bias education for young children and ourselves.* Washington, DC: NAEYC.

Gonzalez-Mena, J. 2010. *50 strategies for communicating and working with diverse families,* 2nd ed. Boston: Pearson.

Kruse, T. S., and Neill, P. 2006. *Multicultural programs.* Ypsilanti, MI: High/Scope Educational Research Foundation.

National Association for the Education of Young Children. 2009. *Where we stand on responding to linguistic and cultural diversity.* Washington, DC: NAEYC.

Office of Head Start. 2010. *Revisiting and updating the multicultural principles for Head Start programs serving children ages birth to five: Addressing culture and home language in Head Start program systems and services.* Washington, DC: U.S. Department of Health and Human Services, Administration for Children & Families, Office of Head Start.

REFLECTION QUESTIONS

- Which resource listed in this chapter will help you most in building your own cultural and linguistic responsiveness?

- What activities will encourage your colleagues and/or staff to improve their cultural and linguistic awareness?

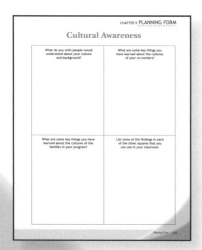

Planning Form

What do you wish people would understand about your culture? What have you learned about the cultures of families in your program? Have staff members share and gain understanding from each other. Use the planning form on page 113 to gather this information.

Multicultural and Multilingual Books

What questions should we ask when choosing linguistically and culturally appropriate books for infants and toddlers?

FOCUS QUESTIONS

- What languages can you find in the board books, cloth books, teacher-made books, and picture books in your program? Do you have a good selection in every language you need?

- Take a look at the messages and pictures in those books. Do you find any stereotypes? Are different skin tones, environments, and clothing represented? Or do you notice that your baby books have no reflection of cultural diversity? What should you add to your collection?

Books are important for infants and toddlers. Books are important for dual language learners. Books are important for early learning. No wonder we devote a whole chapter just to the topic of books! This chapter will focus on two goals: first, to show the reader how to select and evaluate appropriate books for multilingual/multicultural infants and toddlers, and second, to talk about best practices for reading those books to bilingual young children.

When Miss Kim first became an infant/toddler teacher, she was excited to get out a box of her storybooks from her childhood. As she went through the box, she began to realize some of the books that she used to enjoy now looked inappropriate—they had pictures that looked like stereotypes of different races and cultures. So, she took a trip to the library to get some ideas of baby books that show appropriate diversity for her new classroom.

To begin our look at books, let's review the precursors to literacy that book-reading activities support for infants and toddlers.

- Phonemic awareness—playing with the sounds that make up words

- Book knowledge—getting to know how books work

  - Print awareness—beginning to notice that those symbols on the page mean something to the reader

    - Listening skills—experiencing speech sounds in different languages

    - New and higher-level words—building vocabulary

    - Growing persistence and attention span

    - And an extra dose of cuddling that contributes to the nurturing relationship between caregiver and child

    Keeping these objectives in mind will help infant and toddler caregivers understand the importance of choosing the best books. Following are some ideas of what to look for and think about as you make your selections.

LOOK FOR:

- Wordless picture books that allow a story to be told in any language

- Photographs of faces with different-colored skin and different features

- Photographs of everyday things the children can relate to

- Simple artwork with strong lines that represents the artwork of the children's cultures

- Books with two languages on each page

- Books that come in several languages

- Books with realistic situations that can help children understand the world around them

- Books with silly situations for toddlers

- Books with images of the cultures you need but no stereotypes or cartoonish depictions

- Simple, authentic stories rather than American commercial books with licensed characters

- Stories and settings that relate to the actual backgrounds of the children who will see them. For example, not all children from Mexico grew up on farms. Not all children with dark skin will identify with African tribesmen. Not all children who were born in America eat at hamburger chains.

THINK ABOUT:

- Consider asking members of your diversity committee (see chapter 11) or parents to send to their home countries for authentic children's books.

- Always read through every book before placing it in your library—even when the books are in different languages—to make sure each one is of high quality.

- Books you make with photos of your children and their families and their communities can be the best books of all.

The books you choose to use with diverse infants and toddlers can set the stage for learning, interaction, and the tolerant atmosphere in your environment. Aim for high-quality books that both you and the children can enjoy. Ideally, you will collect enough books that you can create a lending library that families also can use. If you have trouble finding books in the languages you need, ask your local public library for help. They often have access to catalogs we never see, and they may have funding to order books that you can borrow to use with your children. Another trick is to have some of the key words of your books translated into the languages you need, then print out the new words on labels and stick them in the books so the reader can use some relevant home-language words with the children who need them.

There are other good reasons to have plenty of bilingual books on hand: They make a great language-learning tool for caregivers, too. In fact, if you can find books that come with CDs, you can load those into an mp3 player, a CD player, or your car stereo and practice the language. The words and phrases you find in children's books usually fit the kinds of things you want to talk about with young children—unlike the typical college or online language course. In addition, you will want to have plenty of books available for volunteers and bilingual staff to read with the children.

It is a good idea to go through your bookshelves and weed out inappropriate or stereotyped books. Ideally, there should be at least 10 books per child and per language available at any time. For infants, these can be cardboard, cloth, or plastic books. Toddlers can use those same books plus paperback and hardcover picture books. Wooden book-display racks that sit low and show the covers of the books, allowing the children to reach and select books themselves, would be ideal. Pay attention to the changing needs of the children. Keep certain favorite books, but change the rest of the selection when you see that some books no longer interest the children. And if you do not have the funds for expensive book shelves, make your own. You may be surprised to learn that disposable diaper cartons make great bookcases— and they can be easily moved and decorated.

Look for books that have repeating words or refrains to help children (and you) become familiar with the vocabulary. Be prepared to read favorite books over … and over … and over again. You might get bored, but young children crave repetition. The brain needs this valuable experience to process information and make connections, especially for young children learning a new language, because they are building new concept knowledge and new sound-and-meaning connections while also learning the stories.

> *Ideally, there should be at least 10 books per child and per language available at any time.*

Try this idea, which is adapted from *Story S-t-r-e-t-c-h-e-r-s for Infants, Toddlers, and Twos: Experiences, Activities, and Games for Popular Children's Books* by Shirley Raines, Karen Miller, and Leah Curry-Rood. Start by reading the book *Baby Faces* by Margaret Miller, a picture book with close-up photographs of babies' faces.

Activity: Magazine Faces

Cut out pictures of children's faces from magazines, glue the pictures to cardboard, and laminate the pictures. Use the pictures to talk about and learn about faces.

Dual language adaptation: Choose key words in the languages of the children in your care, and print out sticky labels with those words to add to the magazine pictures so you can practice naming the features of the face or the emotions displayed using the home languages of the children. Learn "Head, Shoulders, Knees, and Toes" in the other languages of your children, and use that song while they are showing interest in the pictures.

Another way to help dual language learners make sense of stories in their new language is by emphasizing the different characters and events with different voices and tones. This is a case when silliness is actually a sound educational technique! Add to everyone's understanding by using gestures or props—more appropriate with older infants and toddlers—to emphasize the functional meanings of words.

Also, you might consider a somewhat controversial strategy: The Internet offers interesting resources that may fill some needs of young dual language learners, including bilingual children's ebooks in many languages. They may be available in regular ebook format or as applications with narration in different languages, as well as music, animation, or activities.

Many experts advise against screen time for children younger than the age of two, but this may prove to be an exception. Technology should not replace any real books. On the other hand, you can cuddle with a toddler learning English and enjoy a story in English or the child's home language, using the recording to help you repeat pronunciations while touching the different pictures and talking about what you see.

How Do Reading Practices Change as Children Develop?

0–2 months: A newborn baby pays most attention to the sounds of the language spoken by her mother before she was born—a good time to welcome her to your care by learning some of the songs, rhymes, and stories used by her mom.

2–6 months: Before infants can sit on their own, they enjoy being cuddled and engaging in "conversation" with you about books. It is not necessary to read through a whole book. Use it as a guide to talk about the different images and words. Use the names of the baby and her family members.

6–12 months: Now the infant can sit, roll, creep, crawl, and cruise. Try lying on the floor with her and looking at a book together. Children this age are also adept at grabbing things and putting them in their mouths—so have a supply of appropriate books on hand to read and talk about . . . and chew.

12–18 months: Walkers love to grab books and carry them around—try giving them a bag to put the books in, then prepare to have a few reading moments when they pause for a rest. Toddlers at this stage may understand hundreds of words and can say a growing number of words as well, making this a good time to teach them about pointing to objects in a book and saying the words. They also begin to appreciate rhymes and repetition, so capture their attention in that way.

18–30 months: As toddlers begin building sentences, they start to appreciate a whole book and the story in it. They may have a number of favorites at this age, and you likely will see them imitating you by holding a book (often upside down) and pretending to read out loud. That is a sure sign that you and the parents are doing a great job. At this stage, you can begin to point to the actual words you say and to introduce the child to the idea that you are saying words in response to what is written on the page. They also begin to understand what is real and what is pretend. Ask open-ended questions, talk about how the characters feel, and talk about how elements of the story apply to your past or future.

The national organization Zero to Three offers several suggestions to encourage parents to do more reading with their infants and toddlers:

- Choose predictable times so the child knows she can always expect a story at bedtime, on the bus, or when waiting for a ride, a doctor's appointment, or restaurant food.

- Have fun; be silly.

- It is okay if you do not read every page in order—or if you do not finish.

- You do not have to read the words—you can use the book to sing a song or tell a story or just talk about the pictures.

- Let children have some access to books they can choose and pretend to read by themselves.

- Show toddlers the main words—run your finger along the words as you read so they begin to get the idea that your reading is related to the print.

- Make the story interesting with different voices and tones.

- You can even make the story relate to the child by using her name, family names, or the names of her pets.

Keep in mind that young children can benefit quite a bit from listening to stories read in another language. Whether you read a book in English to your dual language learners or read a book in one of the other languages to your English-speaking children, they all gain valuable early-language and literacy experiences. Always begin by orienting the children to the topic of the book using their home languages. Once they have an idea about what to expect, it is okay to read the whole book in the other language. Be sure to use plenty of expression and silly voices, and demonstrate the action to bring the story to life.

Just as we recognize that growing up bilingual contributes to lifelong cognitive, social, and career advantages for children of immigrant families, the same advantages should be supported for children born to English-speaking parents.

They need opportunities to learn the languages of their friends and their communities as well. So, sometimes you will read books in English, and sometimes you will read them in the other languages of the class. Celebrate the wealth of diversity you share with the children.

REFLECTION QUESTIONS

- How can you use books for infants and toddlers to get them started right with a broad and accepting view of cultural and linguistic differences?

- What are some resources in your community that would help you build your multilingual, multicultural library for children and families?

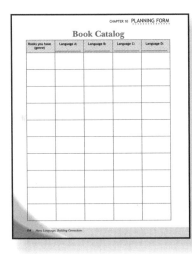

Planning Form

Catalog the books you already have in your classrooms, sorting by genre (e.g., books about animals) and languages. Use the planning form on page 114 to determine what books you need to add to your collection.

The Village, the Community, the Diversity Team

Who is on your diversity team?

FOCUS QUESTIONS

- What questions do you have about the different languages and cultures in your program that you have difficulty finding answers to?

- What members of the community are helpful to you in providing care for infants and toddlers? Could these same helpers add to your knowledge of diversity services in your area?

This chapter takes us beyond the familiar saying, "It takes a village to raise a child," and considers what resources you need to help you support the diverse children in your care and who you need to participate on your "diversity team." Every early childhood program or provider should bring together a diversity team to create a network of support and resources that will ensure the best possible care for young children and their families who come from different language backgrounds. Who can be part of it? What can they do for you and your program?

After Miss Kim visited the local library, she found some good examples of culturally appropriate baby books in English and Spanish, but she was not able to find books showing the Japanese culture, which would be important to two of the children in her group. She asked the school's diversity team to help her find or make storybooks in English and Japanese. One of the team members reached out to a Japanese professor at the local college, who got family members to mail some new books from Japan right to Miss Kim's classroom.

When you bring together members of the community to support your program, you give them a sense of belonging that can make them feel like part of the family. This encourages them to advocate for your program and do their best to help you succeed. Having this team also broadens your access to materials, funding, or other resources that can help with the different languages in your program. Other ways they can help include making items you need, volunteering to translate or interpret, and helping dual language families access educational, employment, or crisis services. Parents who participate have a sense of contributing to their child's program, and experienced bilingual parents make wonderful greeters when a new family comes to the program.

So who could serve on your diversity team? Many religious-education, school-based, or after-school programs require students to engage in community service. Their bilingual participants could be volunteer language buddies or readers in your program. Colleges may have ESL majors looking for internships. The options are endless. The form on page 115 provides some examples of community members who might be part of your diversity team.

REFLECTION QUESTIONS

- Make a list of the languages in your program. Can you identify potential members of your diversity team who can help with each of those languages?

- Create a wish list so that current and potential members of your diversity team will know immediately how they can help make a difference. What's on your list?

- Can you find another infant/toddler care program or other type of organization in your area that already has a diversity team? What can you learn from their experiences?

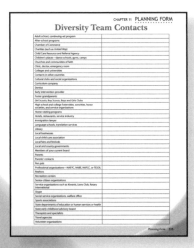

Planning Form

Use the form on page 115 to list contacts in any of these categories that you can find in your local area. Ask these contacts to either serve on your diversity team or to share their knowledge with your diversity team.

chapter 12

Training Bilingual Parents, Volunteers, and Staff

Now that they want to be engaged, how can we help bilingual adults succeed in working with infants and toddlers?

FOCUS QUESTIONS

- Bilingual staff members can be a wonderful asset to any program. What coursework or training have your bilingual staff members had in using their two languages effectively with infants and toddlers?

- What do you expect of volunteers and parents when they come in?

Many programs respond to growing diversity by recruiting and employing bilingual caregivers, assistants, staff, and volunteers, a wonderful and much-needed trend. After you bring people with language assets on board, then what? Is it enough to bring bilingual people in and just set them loose in your program, hoping they know what to do with their two languages? Bilingual teachers regularly report that they receive no professional development or information about what they should do with their language abilities once hired. We often forget that volunteers need training and preparation, too.

The following list offers topics to cover in professional development for bilingual staff and volunteers who will work directly with young children.

Training Points for Bilingual Staff and Volunteers

- Be clear that developmentally appropriate, high-quality interactions with infants and toddlers are the foundation for all of their work.

- Understand the importance of using quality words and sentences in both languages to make the language rich and engaging.

- Provide professional development materials in the other languages. If we want bilingual staff to use high-quality language, we need to support a high level of continuing professional growth in those languages.

- Develop a program phrasebook, and ask bilingual staff to help with translations so all can share important information. (Do not assume that anyone who can speak two languages will make 100 percent accurate translations—always have more than one reader for any translated document to ensure correct and appropriate language.)

- Use the home language with passion, caring, and excitement so that it provides an attractive and enriching model for dual language learners.

- Make lots of eye contact with the children, and get down on their level to establish focused communication and build the relationships.

- Learn how to watch children for cues that help you know how to adjust your interactions with them. Are they showing you they understand? Are they frustrated? Are they interested in something else? Infants and toddlers are excellent nonverbal communicators if you know how to observe and interpret the cues they provide.

- Use touch—but carefully and being respectful of the different levels of comfort shown by each child. Always make sure to follow the program's written guidelines regarding appropriate touch.

- Learn about joint focus—sharing visual connection with the child—and focus your language on what captures the child's attention.

- Practice the rules of good conversation, and take turns with the children, rather than just talking at them. Even young infants enjoy this type of give and take.

- Use open-ended questions. This is one of the most common pieces of advice given to early childhood educators, so make sure staff and volunteers really understand what open-ended questions are and why they matter. Focus on thinking of questions that will lead to further talk and increased interest, as well as offer challenges and discovery.

- Speak clearly and slowly, emphasizing different parts of words.

- Talk most about the here and now so children can relate to your words. Then, as you get to know the child's progress in language development, begin to add conversations about more distant topics like what happened yesterday or what she will do when she goes home tonight.

- Keep language for discipline, behavior management, or control to a minimum. The focus should stay on communication and building relationships. Learn how to use redirection techniques so you can help children cooperate without negative interactions.

- Get comfortable sharing your feelings and experiences. Develop an authentic, special relationship with each child wherein you learn about each other.

- Respect confidentiality. Many times, a bilingual staff member must be called in to help a family understand a delicate matter, and he or she might participate in very private conversations. It is imperative that confidentiality remains a high priority in your program.

- Learn about the curriculum and schedule used by the program. Employers should never assume that new staff or volunteers know how they do things, even if the new person has experience in a similar program. A bilingual volunteer can be an asset to any multilingual program, but sending him in to help without sharing information about what happens in your program and what you expect makes it very difficult for that volunteer to have a successful experience. With a little preparation, every volunteer can enhance your program.

- Collaborate on interactions with parents. Many times, the new staff member who speaks the language of some of the parents will find that she does most of the talking with those parents, and that can set up a separation between teachers. Make sure that all caregivers get to know the parents and have opportunities to chat and share ideas together.

- Practice good reading skills. Because many volunteers come in to read books with the children, take the time to teach them how to do it in the best way. (See chapter 10 on this topic for details.)

- Remember the general rule in multilingual programs: "No simultaneous translations." It is better to read or play in one language and then explain or repeat in the other language at another time. When young children hear information in two languages at the same time, they likely will pay attention to the language that is easier for them and will tune out the new language. Introduce key words and topics of books, games, or songs in the other languages so children are ready for what's to come—but then try to stick to one language during the activity.

- Contribute your many talents and interests to the program—you are more than just another language. Bilingual staff and volunteers can teach everyone songs and games they remember from their childhood traditions. They can bring in clothing, decorations, and hobbies that will help broaden everyone's global perspective.

> *Learn how to use redirection techniques so you can help children cooperate without negative interactions.*

- Support a culturally sensitive and responsible atmosphere throughout the program, within the context of high-quality, developmentally appropriate practices. This means that all staff and volunteers must follow ethical guidelines as well as the policies of your particular program. It helps for bilingual partners to share their cultural understanding, but everyone has to know the boundaries. For example, a volunteer might spoon-feed a 12-month-old because that is common practice in her culture; however, you might be focusing on self-help skills for that child. Is this a case where you might be willing to compromise?

- When the director or administrator of a program does not speak or understand all of the languages being used, she faces many challenges to her traditional supervisory role. Supervisors need to adapt to the changing context by using more observation time to see what behavior reveals. Teach caregivers how to use self-assessments to guide their practice, but avoid having employees report on each other's performance.

A manual or training can cover these key points. Develop them in the context of your program, so the information fits exactly. The planning chart on page 116 provides a format to gather the information needed to prepare bilingual staff and volunteer guidelines that will work for you.

Ana's mom was asked to volunteer in her daughter's child care room. She realized she had never spent a day in an infant/toddler room, and she felt nervous, wondering what she would do. The center director invited her and a couple of other new volunteers to lunch one day. They observed the classrooms and talked informally about how important it is to hold the babies and talk to them in their home language. The director asked the participants to visit different websites where they could view brief videos showing ideas for reading to and singing with bilingual infants and toddlers. By the time she arrived for her first volunteer day, Ana's mom felt confident and ready to help out with her own language.

REFLECTION QUESTIONS

- After reviewing the training topics suggested in this chapter, what topics or information would you add to make sure your parents, staff, and volunteers are prepared to work with you?

- Who can help you in providing training and support of your bilingual participants?

CHAPTER 12   PLANNING FORM

Training Points

Items from "Training Points for Bilingual Staff"	Examples specific to your program	Additional information/ resources needed

Planning Form

Use the form on page 116 to list the training points to cover in your handbook or policies and procedures for bilingual staff and volunteers.

CHAPTER 13

Strategies to Help Caregivers Learn New Languages

What are some easy ways to learn new words to support each baby's home-language development?

FOCUS QUESTIONS

- When you think about learning a new language to connect with an infant or toddler in your care, what challenges or concerns come to mind?

- What might help you or your colleagues overcome objections to learning the languages needed in your program?

Like many early childhood caregivers, Mr. Steve did not speak any Spanish, and languages were hard for him to learn. Yet, the job he applied for was in a center where half of the children came from Hispanic families. The director explained that she understood his hesitation; however, she considered learning the languages of the children in the center just as important as reading, singing, or changing diapers. She invited Mr. Steve to join the Wednesday Spanish Lunch Club, where staff gathered for lunch and spoke only Spanish so they could all practice together in a fun and supportive atmosphere.

Throughout this book—

and most other books about working with young dual language learners—runs the constant reminder that teachers and caregivers must support each child's home language. When faced with this challenge, many American adults react with strong negative emotions. Caregivers want to establish those important language-based connections with the infants and toddlers in their care, but they don't know where to start. Some express a fear of failing or embarrassing themselves. Some remember unpleasant experiences trying to learn languages in high school. Others think they don't have time, or they resent adding a new responsibility to an already-busy schedule. However, if you start from the research-based premise that caregivers need to support the home languages of the babies in their care, then the question changes from *if* they will learn a new language to *how* they will learn it.

First, the director or head teacher needs to acknowledge these negative feelings and address them. If a teacher is concerned that speaking in a new language will make him seem foolish, he needs assurance that everyone is going to learn and try together. If a caregiver's negative attitude gets in the way, she might need more information about the evidence for supporting home languages. Most important, everyone needs to know that they are not being asked to jump into college-level general language courses that will take hours of class time and focus on aspects of the language they will not use in infant/toddler care.

Caregivers for infants and toddlers have many ways to start learning the basic language they need to begin their home-language connections with their charges. Following are 10 recommendations that enable staff to learn some all-important words in each child's home language. Remember to treat all languages with equal respect: We don't want any child left out because his language is less common or not as easy as others.

10 Make a list of 10–20 survival words such as *eat, nap, bathroom, hurt, help, stop,* and *Mommy will be here soon.* Print on a card and send home with a mini-recorder so parents can write and record pronunciations their child will recognize.

9 Get some bilingual children's music. You can find songs on CDs or iTunes that have familiar melodies and use them to learn a few words, such as *hello* and *goodbye,* in the new language.

8 Get songs that you recognize but that are sung entirely in the new language, for additional practice.

7 Slip in to the classroom library area and read the bilingual storybooks when the children are not using them.

6 Find children's books that come with CDs in both languages so you can hear the correct pronunciations, then play them in your car or load them into your music program so you can listen to them on your mp3 player for extra experience.

5 Watch a familiar movie in the new language with English subtitles. If you know the movie well, you'll recognize more of the language in addition to having the English words to help.

4 Play games in other languages, such as Kingka (see kingkagames.com) or ones that come with CDs, so you can learn the words associated with images and practice with adults or children.

3 If you want to practice more advanced Spanish for preschool, order the *Teaching Young Children (TYC)* magazine for teachers from NAEYC.org in English and Spanish (*Tesoros Y Colores*), and stretch your reading ability in both languages.

2 Organize language-learning groups for teachers and staff—maybe everyone can agree to speak only Vietnamese during lunch one day a week.

1 Ask the children! Don't be afraid to try new words, because children love to be the experts who help you learn the right way to say things in their language!

● What words do you already know in other languages? You might surprise yourself with a list that is bigger than you think—and it is your first step to learning a new language.

● How will you use the strategies in this chapter to prepare for each new child?

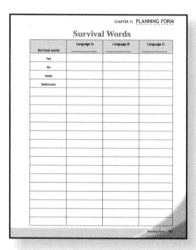

Planning Form

Use the planning form on page 117 to translate "survival words" into the home languages of children at your center.

CHAPTER 14

Supporting Families in Crisis

How can I help families cope with extraordinary needs when they do not speak much English?

FOCUS QUESTIONS

- If you experienced a sudden financial, housing, or health crisis, where would you seek help in your community?

- How would you face that type of challenge if you did not speak the majority language in your community?

One of the infants in the group seemed a bit too fussy—overly sensitive and crying for what seemed like no reason at all. When baby Gina arrived at the child care wearing the same clothes for the third day in a row, the caregiver knew something was going wrong at home, but it was hard to understand Gina's home language, so the caregiver was not able to get much information. She remembered, though, that the local Child Care Resource and Referral Agency (find one near you at naccrra.org) had resources in the different languages of the community. She called and was given the contact information for one of their counselors who spoke Italian, as well as some brochures prepared for the Italian immigrant families in that community about where to go to get different kinds of help.

Noted authority on early childhood education for dual language learners Linda Espinosa says, "When young children are growing up in households that struggle daily with having enough money to buy food, medical care, basic housing, and household supplies, they are also more likely to experience neglect, abuse, and excessive stress or trauma. These multiple influences of an impoverished early learning environment can threaten healthy development" (2009). On the other hand, she points out that "these adverse effects of poverty can be overcome when children have the opportunity to participate in high-quality early childhood programs."

If you serve children from disadvantaged homes, providing stability in your program becomes of the utmost importance. Assign each child her own caregiver, and support that relationship to the maximum extent. Pay extra attention to the specific skills the baby needs to learn and practice, and provide many stimulating opportunities to do so. Emphasize tasks and activities that foster self-regulation and self-determination. Give the children plenty of choices to make and plenty of chances to learn to control their own behavior and activities.

The U.S. Census shows that children younger than the age of six who come from immigrant families form the fastest-growing segment of our population. Some estimates say that close to 25 percent of infants and toddlers in the United States are growing up in homes with languages other than English. We also know that "minority" languages will become "majority" languages in more cities in the coming years. In light of this information, it is important to remember that not all dual-language families are alike.

Espinosa reports that, as of 2007, 13 percent of European-language families (non-Spanish-speaking) and 18 percent of Asian-speaking families fell into the lowest 20 percent of our population for income. For Spanish-speaking families, however, the number is quite shocking: 44 percent of those families were in the lowest income group. That is about three times as high as for English speakers. So when we consider the needs of families in crisis, we cannot lump all dual-language families in the same category. This also means that families who speak Spanish face a greater likelihood of needing supports for themselves and their children—yet the availability of those supports in Spanish remains rare.

Although we can see from these statistics that families who speak Spanish are more likely than other families to live in poverty, this does not mean that every Hispanic family is poor. In fact, 9 percent of Spanish-speaking families sit in the very highest income brackets. So keep in mind the importance of not making assumptions about any one family. In addition, remember that *any* family may be going through a crisis at any given time, regardless of income or socioeconomic status. Caregivers for infants and toddlers need to develop the skill of watching for signs of family stress, because babies cannot explain things. If the family speaks little English, they cannot give you details, either. However, the effects of family

> *If you serve children from disadvantaged homes, providing stability in your program becomes of the utmost importance.*

stress on the developing infant's brain, health, learning ability, mental health, and language are of great concern.

What signs can you look for that might indicate family stress and a need for resources or supports?

- Noticeable changes—parents start arriving late or have someone else drop off the baby

- Appearing distracted—parents start forgetting important items for the baby's day or forgetting payments or required forms

- Changes in appearance—the baby or the parents look especially tired or lose weight

- Changes in behavior—listlessness or fussiness in the child; irritability or depression in the parent

- New symptoms or signs of health problems in the baby

- Changes in dress or personal hygiene—the baby appears wearing the same clothes two days in a row

- Absenteeism—often families drop out of sight when they need you the most

When you notice these or other signs that the family faces trouble, the child's welfare depends on your ability to stay connected. Establishing a positive relationship with each family from the very beginning will pave the way for you to help the families during difficult times. If you have not built that rapport already, getting close to them when they are in trouble becomes highly unlikely.

Use the planning form on page 118 to gather contact information for every resource available in your community, and indicate which ones offer services or information in which languages. You might even offer to share your results with all of the participating agencies so they can all network together. An additional benefit of conducting such a survey is that you can use the opportunity to let the other agencies know you have families who speak other languages and who may need support, so they can plan accordingly.

Do not wait for parents to ask you for help—many people find asking the most difficult challenge of all. Create a list of resources, and let every parent know where to find it if they need it. One program hosted a family fun fair at its site. They had food, music, magic acts, and activities for the children and families. Service agencies from the town ran the booths, and the police department took ID photos for free. The welfare agency did face-painting, the dental clinic handed out free toothbrushes, the library gave away books and signed people up for cards, and the early intervention agency gave out treats. Families came for the fun, but they learned in a nonthreatening way about all the services available to them.

When your observations make you suspect that a family may be in crisis, the staff member closest to the family should try to reach out to them. This must be done in private and with absolute respect. If this effort does not succeed, the director may need to step in.

If you depend on bilingual staff members to handle these difficult situations, then it becomes critical that they receive training. Just because someone speaks two languages does not mean that person is a natural-born social worker! Many programs offer to allow a bilingual staff member to accompany the family to an appointment to help them understand what is happening. This can be a great source of comfort and support. In complex legal proceedings, however, the family will need a certified interpreter.

Did you think, when you signed on to work with infants and toddlers, that you would become part of the support system for the whole family? This may compose a smaller or a larger part of your work—but every infant/toddler caregiver needs to prepare for when emergencies come up. The youngest children are the most vulnerable and need the quickest response to any crisis. You can be the most helpful if you know in advance what people and resources in the community can help in various situations.

REFLECTION QUESTIONS

- How might you pursue an ongoing relationship with multilingual community services in your area so that you can stay up-to-date about what is available and what is new to help families?

- How can you make this support information available to families in the most respectful and comfortable way?

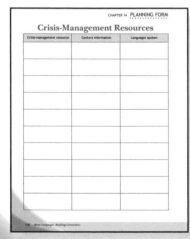

Planning Form

Use the planning form on page 118 to organize the contact information for crisis-management resources and what languages are spoken at each.

CHAPTER 15

Bilingual Infants and Toddlers with Special Needs

What do I need to know to care for infants and toddlers who have disabilities and who are exposed to more than one language?

FOCUS QUESTIONS

- When a small child comes to you from a different home language, how can you determine whether any concerns about his language development are due to his different language or to a true language delay?

- How do personal attitudes, stereotypes, and misinformation affect the planning and implementation of intervention strategies for young DLLs with special needs?

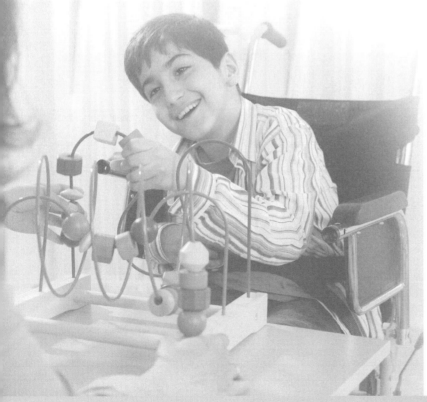

Children are born into families that speak two or more languages every day, all over the world, and some of those children will also have some kind of special need. The good news is that the brains of infants and toddlers can adapt to learning two languages—regardless of any challenges or disabilities they may have. We suggest using a strength-based approach, focusing on what infants and toddlers can do and how caregivers can collaborate with families to help each child reach his potential. A child identified as needing early intervention is a child first—a treasured member of a family who loves him and has hopes and dreams for his future.

If you, the parents, or the child's physician notice the child is not developing as expected in areas related to language, do some careful observations. Children experiencing true language delay or disorder will show it in both of their languages equally. This will be true whether they have delays in expressing language or delays in understanding language. If the child seems to show delays or gaps in one language but normal progress in the other, the issues likely do not indicate a true disorder. Never jump to conclusions about a child's language abilities based only on observations of his language use in your care. Always discuss with the parents how the child talks at home. You will want to learn more about how many words the child understands and uses, how he communicates in his home language as well as in English, and how his language use changes in different settings or with different people.

When an early intervention service provider diagnoses the needs of a child younger than the age of three, he or she will create an Individualized Family Service Plan (IFSP). This plan describes how services will be provided to both the child and his family to help the child meet functional goals for developmental progress. The goals will cover the child's physical, cognitive, communication, social/emotional, and adaptive development.

Often these services are provided in the child's home, but they may take place in the child care setting as well. This enables both the parents and caregivers to learn the strategies the therapists and specialists use, so everyone can work together to move the child toward those developmental goals. Ideally, the IFSP is written with both the family and the care setting in mind. Professionals involved in providing therapies and services needed by the child might include any of the following:

- Audiologists
- Speech-language pathologists
- Family therapists
- Special educators
- Nurses
- Social workers

- Nutritionists
- Psychologists
- Occupational therapists
- Pediatricians/physicians
- Physical therapists

Caring for a child with special needs may seem like a daunting task, but many of the strategies used by specialists and therapists look a lot like the play, games, and activities you already know. The early intervention staff tries to get to know the family and the caregiver(s) and to tailor the approach so it will work with the culture, resources, and abilities of everyone who will participate in supporting the progress of the baby.

Occasionally, you may encounter a specialist or therapist who believes that learning in two languages is not good for the child with special needs. Experts and researchers have worked hard to explain that this myth has no basis in fact. Paradis, Genesee, and Crago (2010) advise us to "expect children with language or cognitive disabilities to have the capacity to become bilingual, unless there is compelling evidence to the contrary."

Let's consider what the national professional association for early childhood special education, the Council for Exceptional Children, Division for Early Childhood (CEC-DEC), has to say on this topic:

Children and families come to early intervention with different ways of behaving and communicating. Therefore, intervention planning and implementation should incorporate the family's language and culture to support and honor family practices. Dual language learners, including those children with disabilities, should be afforded the opportunity to maintain their home language while also learning English, as there is no scientific evidence that being bilingual causes or leads to language delay. Supporting a child's home language in fact acts as a linguistic resource and bridge to learning another language, even for children with disabilities. Research confirms that immersing DLLs fully in English when they are still in the active process of learning their home language actually has negative ramifications such as the inability to communicate with parents and relatives, preference for English, and depressed academic and reading achievement in English in later school years.

The home language builds the foundation for that all-important bond with parents and family, making it one of the most important reasons to continue supporting the first language for infants and toddlers in your care. We know that strong family relationships and family involvement in school are key factors in ensuring the child's eventual graduation and success into adulthood. Would you say that children with special needs depend on that family support any less than other children? Certainly not! In fact, we realize that working with young children with special needs requires a strong partnership with their parents. Those children need a strong family base to help them weather the challenges they face.

The CEC-DEC position paper also emphasizes the importance of honoring the culture of the family. As we have said before, language is embedded in culture. To properly support a child's home language, one has to recognize the home culture as well. That does not mean knowing what country the child comes from; it means getting to know the family and honoring their points of view, traditions, and values. When writing an Individual Family Service Plan for the infant or toddler with special needs, specialists should consider the culture and the language of the family to create an effective plan.

Ten-month-old Pablo was still not able to sit up on his own. Despite a bit of a language barrier, Miss Cary talked to the parents, but they told her that it was part of their culture to carry babies all the time and that must be why he wasn't sitting up. Miss Cary watched a video of typically developing 10-month-olds and realized there were a few other skills that Pablo hadn't accomplished yet. By showing the video to the parents, she could communicate her concerns and help them connect with a bilingual intake worker at the early intervention program.

The ease of therapeutic strategies for infants and toddlers with language delays or disorders might surprise you, and any of these strategies can take place in English as well as in the child's home language.

If a baby is diagnosed with delays in listening or understanding language (also called *receptive language*), a speech-language pathologist might recommend strategies such as:

- Reading a brief story to the baby and asking him to show you or point to the items in the pictures.
- While playing with the baby, ask him to perform an action such as handing you the cup or rolling the ball, to encourage him to respond to your words.

If the child has delays in talking and using language (also called *expressive language*), recommendations might include:

- Using traditional songs that ask the child to say a predictable part.

- During diaper changes, modeling good language by talking about the things you are using and what you are doing.

In many cases, early intervention will include the use of sign language to support the young child's language development and ability to communicate. This is generally a very useful strategy for children who have been frustrated by their inability to let others know what they think or feel. When children cannot communicate well with oral language, using signs can help build their communication skills and teach new concepts, allowing their cognitive development to progress while waiting for their language skills to catch up. There is no research to support the old myth that learning sign language will prevent a young child from learning to talk. On the contrary, sign language supports language development and supports the child's bond with his family and caregivers.

Always remember that a dual language learner who also has special needs will benefit from support of his home language and culture as well as support of English. Teaching strategies that benefit any child's language development will also benefit children with delays. Partnering with the specialists and the family to meet the child's special needs can be a rewarding experience for everyone.

> *There is no research to support the old myth that learning sign language will prevent a young child from learning to talk.*

REFLECTION QUESTIONS

- How can you use the information learned in this chapter to work more effectively with bilingual parents of babies who have special needs?

- How might you use this information to support your efforts to advocate for early intervention practices or recommendations that will be linguistically appropriate for a child?

Planning Form

Use the planning form on page 119 to list the resources for children with special needs that are available in different languages. Include assessments, evaluators, therapists, diagnosticians, clinics, and so forth so that you can identify any gaps in your service area.

CHAPTER 16

Infants and Toddlers Adopted from Different Countries

What special considerations do children of international adoptions need?

FOCUS QUESTIONS

- Look for an organization near you that supports families with international adoptions. What can you learn from them about the experiences of families as they adopt from different countries?

- What are the different kinds of stress that might be affecting an infant who has been adopted from another country?

Cho Hee was adopted from Korea when she was 22 months old. She wasn't speaking much in any language, but her caregiver, Miss Kim, knew that Cho Hee probably had learned a lot of Korean already and must be thinking in Korean, too. So, Miss Kim worked with the parents to develop some activities in Korean they could do with Cho Hee in care as well as at home while they also exposed her to rich, engaging English.

When you care for a child who has been adopted from another country, you may develop an entirely new set of questions. With experts strongly recommending that we support a young child's home language, you might wonder what to do if the child's first language differs from the language now spoken in her home. You would have company in wondering that: A number of researchers want to find out how these children resemble other learners of English, how they differ, and what conditions best support their language development.

Young children adopted from other countries commonly come to live with a family who does not speak their first language fluently, if at all. Depending on where they were born and where their new community is, children may not have anyone in the neighborhood who speaks their first language. Typically, everyone focuses on helping the child learn the family's language as soon as possible, and the first language fades. If the adopted child is younger than the age of two, this becomes almost like developing a second "first language."

The age of the child appears important in determining the success of the language transition. Children who enter the new family language environment after the age of two will more likely encounter some lasting effects that may slow their language development or interfere with their success in school. When the adoption occurs before the child is six months old, we expect that the change of language will not have a noticeable long-term effect.

However, there are conflicting findings about what happens to the language progress of children adopted between the ages of six months and 24 months. Many factors come into play. Some studies seem to show that a child adopted during this time period who loses her home language may show some early language delay. Other findings indicate that she may start out with seemingly normal progress in the new language, but learning difficulties may appear later as she goes through elementary school. Still other studies have found that some children develop normally as they weather this

> *Young children adopted from other countries commonly come to live with a family who does not speak their first language fluently, if at all.*

significant life change. Regardless, children adopted after the age of six months clearly can benefit from enhanced language-development supports. Many of the strategies contained in the earlier chapters will help caregivers and parents ensure that the child experiences a rich, supportive foundation to make the most of her innate ability and temperament.

Other factors that will affect the progress of the adopted child include general health, nutrition, and the quality of the language environment before adoption. There may be a connection between the similarities shared by the child's first and second languages and the ease of the transition. You may not know whether the child was developing normally in her first language or whether she was experiencing delays. We should also look into the resources available to the new family as they support their child through this transition. Some families make an effort to learn some of the child's first language and use it with varying levels of success and frequency, but other families believe it is best to move forward and focus on providing high-quality second-language experiences only.

With the potential for such great variation in these areas, it is impossible to draw any general conclusions about the language development of internationally adopted children. Get to know the child and the adoptive parents as individuals and as a family unit, then develop individualized plans to support language development from that base. If the family has chosen to give up the child's first language and is committed to providing a good quality learning environment in the new language, you will want to follow their lead.

The support of the child's home culture arises as an additional source of questions. Again, follow the new family's lead. This underscores the importance of taking the time to understand the values, beliefs, and plans the parents bring to this situation. If the parents decided not to incorporate the child's cultural heritage into their lives, the caregiver should leave out references to the child's other culture to avoid confusion. If the parents decide to maintain elements of the child's original culture, it would be wonderful if you and your program would join with them to learn and use some of these elements. (Look for strategies in the earlier chapters to help you think of ways to learn about the culture and find materials for your program.)

REFLECTION QUESTIONS

- What information from this chapter would you like to include in a brochure for new parents who have adopted their babies from other countries?

- How can you use this information to design interview questions that help you get to know the history and wishes of adoptive families?

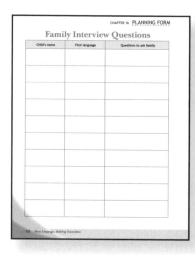

Planning Form

Use the planning form on page 120 to list the children in your center who were adopted from different countries and their country of origin. Develop interview questions to ask their parents about their emphasis on maintaining original culture and/or language.

CHAPTER 17

Stages, Standards, and Expectations

What do we want bilingual babies to know and to be able to do?

- What are the standards or rules that you are expected to follow in your program that relate to language and cultural differences?

- Do you use program or developmental assessments that are linguistically and culturally appropriate?

Every state has standards for what school-aged children should learn, but at this writing, only a handful of states have written standards for what infants and toddlers should know and be able to do. In some states, guidance about best practices for infants and toddlers is found in different departments that may or may not be coordinated. The state department of education, the department of health, the department of human services (or similar offices that oversee child care licensing), or the department that supports families and deals with institutional or family child-abuse cases—any of these may address infant/toddler care and development. Programs that receive funding from these different agencies may have additional rules based on their contracts. In addition, many organizations must also comply with rules that come with private funding or national funding.

The strategies in this book are meant to support and enhance the guidance that is most prevalent—from state standards, the Office of Head Start, and other national leadership organizations. It is important, however, to keep up with changes both at the local level and the national level. Many states are developing new infant/toddler guidelines as the field receives more attention. Using the strategies in this book will enable you to modify your practices to meet updated state and national recommendations while making those recommendations work effectively with the culturally and linguistically diverse children and families in your care.

Let's look at some examples of state standards for infant and toddler care and development.

The Maryland Department of Education's *Healthy Beginnings* (2010) guidelines include hundreds of indicators/examples organized into four domains: Personal and Social Development, Language Development, Cognitive Development, and Physical Development. Each domain breaks down into eight age groups, from birth through three years. Their guidelines do not mention any adaptations for children who come from different home languages. Caregivers can use what they have learned in this book to take a second look at the indicators and think about how they will work with children who have not been exposed to your language. For example, the Language Development guidelines say that a child aged four months to eight months should "show more interest in speech—Respond to one-step direction, such as 'Come to mommy,'—Point to the cat in a book when you say, 'Where is the cat?'"

A child new to your language may not show much interest in your speech at first, making it important to observe him in interactions with family members or others who do speak the language he is used to. By observing family interactions and talking with the parents, you will learn more about what that infant knows and can do in his home language. If you find out that the baby crawls to his mommy when she says, "*Ven con mamá*," then you shouldn't expect him to crawl to you when you say those words in English. Learn to say phrases in his language so you can build on that existing skill and knowledge, then transition to saying them in English.

However, if you show the child a new book that he hasn't seen before, and you suspect that he hasn't already learned the word *elephant* in his home language, you might go ahead and introduce the book to him in English and talk to him about the elephants in the picture. Then, you expect him to point correctly when you say, "Point to the elephant," in English. To interact effectively with dual language learners in the first few years, each caregiver must interpret standards in each situation, using his or her professional judgment to be flexible, creative, and responsive to each child's needs.

Pennsylvania has taken an innovative approach by connecting the departments of education and welfare to create the Office on Child Development and Early Learning. That office developed *Learning Standards for Early Childhood—Infants—Toddlers* (2009). It contains the following standards areas:

- Approaches to Learning Through Play

- Creative Thinking and Expression

- Cognitive Thinking and Knowledge: Mathematical Thinking and Expression, Scientific Thinking, and Technology and Social Studies Thinking

- Health, Wellness, and Physical Development

- Language and Literacy Development

- Partnerships for Learning

- Social and Emotional Development

It has standards for infants, young toddlers, and older toddlers with examples, and the document suggests supportive practices for each standard, as well as incorporating supports for English-language learners throughout. For example, under Home-School Connections, the standards document contains this recommendation, "Add culturally specific materials and experiences into the schedule and environment, such as adding a wok to the cooking area, or counting in both English and Spanish during morning message."

Delaware also has developed guidance for infant/toddler caregivers. It offers the *Delaware Infant and Toddler Early Learning Foundations: A Curricular Framework* (2006), which talks about what the child should be able to do and what the teacher should do in support. Its domains include language development, social and emotional development and attachment, motor development, cognitive discovery, and the well-being of the parents and caregivers. Although it does not give any explicit guidance about dual language learners, it does offer some ideas such as, "Provide multicultural, diverse materials (books, dolls, music, and dramatic play), role play, and talk about the similarities and differences."

New Hampshire provides early childhood standards under its Preschool Special Education Office and adds infant and toddler behaviors as precursors to the benchmarks listed for preschool students. The domains covered by the New Hampshire document are Cognitive Development, Health and Safety, Communication and Literacy Development, Creative Expression and Aesthetic Development, Approaches to Learning, Social and Emotional Development, and Physical Development.

The key language indicators for infants and toddlers that are precursors to the Communication and Literacy Development benchmarks at the preschool level include (quoting from the New Hampshire standards):

- Engaging in face-to-face interactions with others
- Listening and responding to verbal and nonverbal cues
- Repeating sounds purposefully

- Communicating needs, ideas, and thoughts through verbal and nonverbal expression

- Beginning to put sounds together to form words

- Identifying familiar people, places, objects, and actions in everyday life, photos, and books

- Enjoying exploring books and listening to stories

- Beginning to experiment with writing tools

You can see that some details differ from one state model to the next, but overall, the similarities outnumber the differences. It is a major undertaking for state departments to come together and agree upon exactly what infants and toddlers should know and be able to do—not to mention what supports parents, teachers, or caregivers should provide. The addition of adjustments for children from different languages and different cultures is rare.

Because so much of the guidance written about infant/toddler care and development is heavily dependent on language, when you read the guidance available from your state or organization, pay close attention to each item that refers to what children can say or understand. These items may appear in the obvious language/literacy domains, but you will also see examples in other domains. For example, expectations for the child's social development depend on the ability to converse with caregivers and peers. Health and safety items require that the child understand instructions or stop when called. As you work toward enhancing your relationships with the infants and toddlers in your care, consider language differences in every situation and for every purpose.

Age breakdowns constitute one key area of difference among state and organization developmental charts. Some divide by four-month intervals. Some just say, "infant, young toddler, older toddler." Others break down stages by milestones rather than ages. Any infant/toddler development expert will acknowledge the great variability in early development. Knowing the age of the child does not matter as much as knowing *the child*—knowing his capabilities and challenges, his temperament, and his interests.

REFLECTION QUESTIONS

- Use the information from this chapter to write your own program standards for infants and toddlers who are dual language learners.

- How has this chapter helped you look more closely at your program to ensure that each and every child has the opportunity to meet expectations, no matter what his home language is?

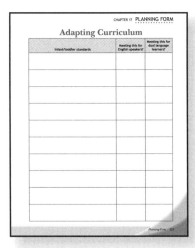

Planning Form

Fill out the planning form on page 121 with the infant/toddler standards that apply to your program, with blanks for checking off how you meet them for children who come from a non-English-speaking home.

Enhancing Infant/Toddler Curriculum for Multiple Languages

We already have a curriculum; how can I make it work in multilingual groups?

FOCUS QUESTIONS

- Do you use a formal curriculum? an informal curriculum? a combination of several curricula? Or would you say you use no curriculum at all?

- What guidance has been provided by any of the curriculum elements you use for adaptations for dual language learners?

A curriculum for infants and toddlers is kind of a funny thing: Many people find it pretty easy to say what that curriculum should *not* look like but not so easy to agree on what it *should*. Many people who care for babies choose no curriculum at all. Infant/toddler curriculum models do not look like those we use for children old enough to read and write. We do not want a curriculum that focuses on preparing the little ones for standardized tests or gives them worksheets. But, what *do* we want?

In *The Comprehensive Infant Curriculum* (2000) Kay Albrecht and Linda G. Miller share their vision for a truly innovative curriculum for young children. They remind us that the curriculum provides teachers with a means to plan activities yet also equips them with enough knowledge about child development and learning that they can respond to the changing needs and interests of the children. Albrecht and Miller advocate for an early curriculum that offers enough structure to support the teacher's goals for each child yet stays open-ended enough to allow each child to shine.

Using their framework, let us take a look at the ways you can adapt an existing early childhood curriculum to meet the different cultural and linguistic needs of the children in your care, while staying true to the nature of the curriculum and all of the benefits that made you adopt it in the first place.

Developmental Tasks

A thorough and dynamic infant/toddler curriculum describes what you can expect children to know and be able to do at each step along their developmental path. This is a helpful place to start when adapting your curriculum for dual language learners. Points to consider include the following:

- For most children, their development during the first two years will follow the same basic path in each of their languages, so they need continuing practice and high-quality input in both languages.

- Some children may slow down for a brief period as they focus on making sense of the two different languages and learn how to keep them apart. This may be followed by a sprint ahead as the stimulation of two languages exercises the brain's language-learning apparatus.

- A bilingual baby may express her cognitive development in one language or the other. She needs a caregiver who knows her very well and can help her use and demonstrate her knowledge in whatever language feels comfortable at the time—even if that is a combination of two languages.

- A child's language development generally plays a role in all other developmental areas, so keeping a close eye on her progress in both languages will help you be more effective in supporting her development in other areas.

Observations and Assessments

Careful observation becomes especially important with linguistically diverse groups of children. You may have a difficult time finding fully unbiased, valid assessments for infants and toddlers in languages other than English. To capture the true knowledge and progress of dual language learners, assessment would have to work equally well in both languages of the child and be without cultural bias. Because that is a rare find, caregivers need to rely much more heavily on very solid observation and recording skills. One of the most important adaptations here is to record the sounds made by the child. This allows you to play the recordings for a colleague or the parent, so they can help you make accurate notes of the child's speech attempts in different contexts.

Child Development

Understanding the major theories of child development gives a caregiver the foundation to understand what a baby needs and how she can support the baby's unique development. When caring for diverse infants and toddlers, you will want to arm yourself with specialized knowledge. The resource list at the end of the book has many entries to support you in your professional development.

Interactive Experiences

Albrecht and Miller highlight the value of child-to-child and child-to-adult interactions as important contributors to the young child's learning experience. Rather than letting these rich learning opportunities go aimlessly by, capitalize on their value and meaning for dual language learners by observing what does happen and then developing curriculum plans to guide interactions as needed. In classrooms of older children, experts advocate grouping children from the same home language together. Even for toddlers, the opportunity for relaxed and engaging conversations with other children who speak the same language can be an important element of your language-development curriculum goals.

Teaching

Teaching goals are an important part of any curriculum. When the children do not speak the same language as the teacher or caregiver, planning has to extend beyond the ordinary expectations.

- Be explicit in your planning for dual language learners. Just as you would write down the activities and materials needed in your lesson plan, you should also write down the actions you will take to support learning for the children who come from different language backgrounds. Write these actions down as part of your plan so you can document the efforts you make on behalf of each child.

- Keep in mind that children need "comprehensible input" to learn. ESL teachers in older grades use this phrase, and it means that teachers should make sure children can understand what they are trying to teach. You can use many of the same strategies adapted for older ESL classes to help children understand what they need to learn when the teacher does not speak their language. Plan ahead so you can communicate key information using the following techniques:

- Gestures
- Modeling and demonstrating
- Pictures
- Props
- Repetition
- Tone of voice
- Translated materials

Meumi has just enrolled in Mr. Joon's toddler class. She speaks a few words of Japanese and no English at all. Mr. Joon felt unprepared to change his curriculum plans for this new member of his group. Then, he started thinking about what he had learned in his storytelling workshop. As he started using more gestures, body movements, and expression to communicate with Meumi, he realized she was not the only one responding. Soon all the children were catching on and seemed to understand more.

- Plan carefully for opportunities to repeat, that is, to build predictability into the learning process. Dual language learners need a heavy dose of this strategy.

- A stable schedule with clear signals helps the children understand what is happening throughout the day. This also supports easy transitions.

- Eye contact and getting on the child's level—key early childhood teacher behaviors—become even more important when you do not know how many of your words the children understand. Just as they use your facial expressions and body language to understand what you say, you will depend on observing the same things to help you understand the children. Build plenty of time into your planned activities so you do not rush through and miss those one-to-one opportunities.

My mom taught early childhood her whole career. Then she retired—and became a volunteer early childhood teacher. No matter that she was in her seventies and had arthritis, whenever she met one of the preschool children from the neighborhood, she would disappear. All of a sudden, she'd be out of sight—and then I would remember to look down because she always dropped to the child's eye level to have a chat!

Parent Participation and Involvement

No one can deny the importance of parent involvement in any infant/toddler program. A strong partnership with parents of dual language learners will make it possible for you to understand and meet the children's needs within your curriculum. Helping parents participate with the learning process at home also can be a significant part of your overall curriculum planning. Do not just build in holiday celebrations or classroom visits that have limited value. Really focus on involving the parents as intentional partners in the curriculum process.

If you do not speak the child's home language fluently, the parent's ability to provide high-quality early language and literacy experiences in that language becomes even more vital for the child who is growing up bilingual. So, as you plan the activities to implement within your curriculum, keep one of the columns in the chart ready to assign tasks to parents on a regular basis, and encourage them to read, talk, sing, explore, and learn with their child in their home language … a lot!

Environment

A curriculum for infant and toddler groups will address the items in the classroom that support the overall learning, experiences, goals, and lesson plans for each day. As we have said before, some level of stability and predictability matters for all babies; and this is especially true for babies who do not understand the language around them. However, too much sameness is not good for babies either. We all know how an infant uses her vocal strength to tell us she is bored! A well-prepared teacher finds a balance in the curriculum between stability and stimulating change. Plan to periodically swap out some materials the children have lost interest in and replace them with specifically chosen, curriculum-related items.

Activities and Experiences

Planning activities and experiences for infants and toddlers can provide a great deal of joy to caregivers who really understand where their children are and where they want them to go. This part of curriculum planning gives creativity a place to flourish and to be documented. Regardless of your creative talents, having the backdrop of a comprehensive curriculum allows you and the children to get the most benefit from your imaginative talents. This also enables you to plan in advance and incorporate the options you require to meet the different language needs of the children. Use the planning form provided on page 122 to get started.

- Were you using any curriculum strategies that you have decided to eliminate after reading this chapter?

- What key points will you keep in mind to adapt future curriculum materials to meet the language needs of the infants and toddlers in your program?

Curriculum Adaptation Planning Chart

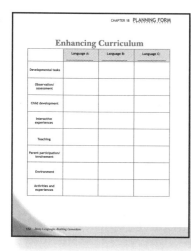

Fill out the form on page 122 with the languages you need across the top, and populate the squares with ideas you have learned from the chapters of this book to help you with curriculum planning.

Adapting Activities from Your Favorite Books

How can we use our favorite infant/toddler activities effectively with children learning in more than one language?

FOCUS QUESTIONS

- Do some of your favorite teaching strategies seem to fall short when working with young dual language learners?

- Which authors do you use most often to add new activities for the infants and toddlers in your care?

This final chapter is designed to bring together everything you have learned from this book and to help you see new ways to put the ideas into action. You do not need to add a dual language learner curriculum on top of the plans you already have for your program. You can adapt any activity or curriculum to meet the needs of infants and toddlers with the resources available to you.

Miss Sholeen is caring for a 10-month-old boy who was just adopted from China last month. She knows that this boy needs especially strong support of his relationship with his new adoptive parents while he is away from them all day in child care. She goes through her collection of songs and rhymes and picks some that specifically mention mommy and daddy, and she makes sure she has several pictures of the new parents on hand to show to him with each song.

Many activities designed for infants and toddlers focus on helping them develop language and provide the kinds of supports that are useful for children learning in one or more languages. The important thing is for you to understand the needs of dual language learners, so you can add features to your chosen activities that will meet those needs. As you think about adapting activities to be effective with infants and toddlers who come from different languages, you can keep in mind some basic recommendations:

- Find some of the key words from the new activity to learn in the child's language.

- Link one activity to another by finding activities that use some of the same words you have learned in other languages—to make it easier for you to support the home language and to give children that important opportunity for repetition and practice.

- Add to the meaning of the activity by adding planned gestures, sign language, pictures, or props.

- Ask families to share similar activities they may enjoy at home, in their home language—or ask them to practice the new activity in their home language.

- Whenever possible, use authentic, real items to support new activities to help infants and toddlers learn new things based on prior learning.

- When you introduce a new activity and adapt it to meet the needs of your DLLs, plan to use it over and over again—giving children and adults plenty of time to understand it and benefit from it.

While you may have many favorites, it is important to pay close attention to the activities, songs, and games you play with each infant and toddler, because these are key opportunities to support their individual needs. Here are some examples based on popular infant/toddler books already available on the market.

From *Games to Play with Babies*, 3rd ed. by Jackie Silberg

Activity: "Good Night Baby" (page 19)
Softly sing a song such as "Twinkle, Twinkle, Little Star" while you feed the baby a bottle. As you sing, gently massage the baby's hands, fingers, feet, and toes.

Dual language adaptation: Choose one language to use during feeding times and be consistent. If you use the home language at that time—be sure you sing the song in the baby's home language, too.

Activity: "Sing, Sing, Sing" (page 109)
Make up words to familiar songs, changing the words to describe what is happening in the baby's environment right now. The words do not have to rhyme, but putting them into a song makes things interesting.

Dual language adaptation: Use this idea to learn and practice words and phrases in the infant's home language.

Activity: "What Toy Is It?" (page 147)

Pick out three of the baby's favorite toys and hold them up, one at a time, saying the name of the toy. Then, ask the baby to pick up one toy, then the next, then the next. This helps him learn the names of the items as well as the idea of responding to your requests.

Dual language adaptation: Use this activity to help the baby practice responding to English vocabulary.

Activity: "Copy Me" (page 225)

Sit on the floor with the baby and encourage him to copy you while you smack the floor, tap your nose, stick out your tongue, wave your hands, and so on. Make sure to do plenty of talking while you do the activities.

Dual language adaptation: This activity will help you and the child practice words and actions together. When you sit down, announce the language you will be using, and stick to that language throughout the activity.

From *Teaching Infants, Toddlers, and Twos with Special Needs* by Clarissa Willis

Activity: "Augmentative Communication" (page 93)

Make pictures of different toys and activities available for children who cannot tell their caregivers and friends what they want. They can point to a picture or hand it to their playmate to establish communication.

Dual language adaptation: Use this strategy to help newcomers communicate— but be sure to narrate their interactions so they hear the words in their home language and English as well.

From *Baby Smarts: Games for Playing and Learning* by Jackie Silberg

Activity: "Bye Bye Light" (page 77)

Let the baby help you turn the light switch off and on, saying, "Bye-bye, light," when you switch the light off so they learn the meaning of the word.

Dual language adaptation: Use this kind of activity to help babies make clear connections between things, actions, or events and the words used for them—in English at some times and in the home language at other times.

REFLECTION QUESTIONS

- Name one or two basic adaptation ideas you learned in this chapter that you could use with any teaching and play ideas you see in articles and books.

Final Words

All babies need to play. They need to explore. They need to pretend. They need to build. They need to make a mess. They need to touch and smell and taste and listen and see. They need to play-act and grow their imaginations.

We believe that all these activities actually contribute to the development of key abilities, such as self-regulation, planning, and problem-solving that will ensure successful outcomes as children go through school. Children who speak more than one language need to have all of these experiences supported through verbal communications in both their home language and their school language, as well as through nonverbal communication. In addition, these aspects of play are vital to the further development of language—both receptive language and expressive language.

Toddlers need lots of opportunities to talk through their play—even if we do not understand what they say. They also need lots of opportunities to interact with other children and adults—providing them with lots of new language they can try. This can happen in the home language or in English—but it must be rich, engaging, and high-quality language in either case. Most important of all, infants and toddlers will thrive in the care of adults who communicate with them in a loving and nurturing way.

Identify Your Challenges

Challenges with staff	Challenges with families	Challenges finding/ obtaining resources	Challenges about professional development

Professional-Development Goals

Professional-development goal	Chapter that gave you the information needed	Plan for unmet professional-development needs

Supporting Multiple Languages

Strategy	Child 1 Home language: _____	Child 2 Home language: _____	Child 3 Home language: _____	Child 4 Home language: _____

Welcoming Diverse Families

Strategies	Language 1 _____	Language 2 _____	Language 3 _____	Language 4 _____

Parent Helpers

Parent	Skills	Task/role

Valuing Diversity

	Language/culture	Have	Need
Displays			
Books			
Props/puppets			
Recorder/camera			
Supports for teacher			
Manipulatives			
Dramatic-play items			

Cultural Awareness

What do you wish people would understand about your culture and background?	**What are some key things you have learned about the cultures of your co-workers?**
What are some key things you have learned about the cultures of the families in your program?	**List some of the findings in each of the other squares that you can use in your classroom.**

Book Catalog

Books you have (genre)	Language A: _____	Language B: _____	Language C: _____	Language D: _____

Diversity Team Contacts

Adult school, continuing-ed program	
After-school programs	
Chamber of Commerce	
Charities (such as United Way)	
Child Care Resource and Referral Agency	
Children's places—dance schools, gyms, camps	
Churches and communities of faith	
Clinic, doctor, emergency room	
Colleges and universities	
Contacts in other countries	
Cultural clubs and social organizations	
Curriculum company	
Dentist	
Early intervention provider	
Foster grandparents	
Girl Scouts, Boy Scouts, Boys and Girls Clubs	
High school and college fraternities, sororities, honor societies, and service organizations	
Home-visiting programs	
Hotels, restaurants, service industry	
Immigration lawyer	
Language schools, translation services	
Library	
Local businesses	
Local child care association	
Local fairs and festivals	
Local and county governments	
Members of your current board	
Parents	
Parents' contacts	
Pen pals	
Professional organizations—NAEYC, NABE, NAFCC, or TESOL	
Realtors	
Recreation centers	
Senior-citizen organizations	
Service organizations such as Kiwanis, Lions Club, Rotary International	
Skype	
Social-service organizations, welfare office	
Sports associations	
State departments of education or human services or health	
State early childhood advisory board	
Therapists and specialists	
Travel agencies	
Volunteer organizations	

Training Points

Items from "Training Points for Bilingual Staff"	Examples specific to your program	Additional information/resources needed

Survival Words

Survival words	Language A: _____	Language B: _____	Language C: _____
Yes			
No			
Hello			
Bathroom			

Crisis-Management Resources

Crisis-management resource	Contact information	Languages spoken

Special Needs Resources

Resources available in your area	Language A: English	Language B: _____	Language C: _____	Language D: _____

Family Interview Questions

Child's name	First language	Questions to ask family

Adapting Curriculum

Infant/toddler standards	Meeting this for English speakers?	Meeting this for dual language learners?

Enhancing Curriculum

	Language A: _____	Language B: _____	Language C: _____
Developmental tasks			
Observation/ assessment			
Child development			
Interactive experiences			
Teaching			
Parent participation/ involvement			
Environment			
Activities and experiences			

References, Resources, and Organizations

References

Albrecht, K., and Miller, L. G. 2000. *The comprehensive infant curriculum.* Beltsville, MD: Gryphon House.

August, D., and Shanahan, T. 2006. *Developing literacy in second-language learners: Report of the National Literacy Panel on language-minority children and youth.* Mahwah, NJ: Lawrence Erlbaum Associates.

Bardige, B. S. 2008. *Talk to me, baby! How you can support young children's language development.* Baltimore, MD: Paul H. Brookes Publishing.

Chang, F., Crawford, G., Early, D., Bryant, D., Howes, C., Burchinal, M., Barbarin, O., Clifford, R., and Pianta, R. 2007. Spanish-speaking children's social and language development in pre-kindergarten classrooms. *Early Education and Development* 18(2): 243–269.

Collier, V. P. 1987. Age and rate of acquisition of a second language for academic purposes. *TESOL Quarterly 6*(21): 617–641.

Council for Exceptional Children, Division for Early Childhood. 2010. Position Statement: *Responsiveness to ALL children, families, and professionals: Integrating cultural and linguistic diversity into policy and practice.* Missoula, MT. dec-sped.org.

Delaware Department of Education. 2006. *Delaware infant and toddler early learning foundations: A curricular framework.* Dover, DE. doe.k12.de.us/infosuites/students_family/earlychildhood/files/earlychildhood_infant-toddler.pdf.

Derman-Sparks, L., and Edwards, J. O. 2010. *Anti-bias education for young children and ourselves.* Washington, DC: NAEYC.

Espinosa, L. M. 2009. *Getting it right for young children from diverse backgrounds: Applying research to improve practice.* Upper Saddle River, NJ: Pearson.

Fortuny, K., Hernandez, D. J., and Chaudry, A. 2010. *Young children of immigrants: The leading edge of America's future.* Washington, DC: The Urban Institute.

Gonzalez-Mena, J. 2010. *50 Strategies for communicating and working with diverse families*, 2nd ed. Boston, MA: Pearson.

Harms, T., Cryer, D., and Clifford, R. 2006. *Infant/toddler environment rating scale*, revised ed. New York: Teachers College Press.

Kohl, M. F. 2002. *First art: Art experiences for toddlers and twos*, Beltsville, MD: Gryphon House.

Kruse, T. S., and Neill, P. 2006. *Multicultural programs*. Ypsilanti, MI: HighScope Educational Research Foundation.

Kuhl, P. 2010. TED (Technology, education, design) videotaped presentation: *The linguistic genius of babies*. ted.com/talks/patricia_kuhl_the_linguistic_genius_of_babies.html.

Maryland State Department of Education. 2010. *Healthy beginnings*. Baltimore: Maryland State Department of Education. marylandhealthybeginnings.org.

National Association for the Education of Young Children. 2009. *Where we stand on responding to linguistic and cultural diversity*. Washington, DC: NAEYC.

Nemeth, K. 2009. Meeting the home language mandate: Practical strategies for all classrooms. *Young Children 64*(2): 36–42.

Office of Child Development and Early Learning. 2009. *Pennsylvania learning standards for early childhood: Infants–toddlers*, 2nd ed. Harrisburg, PA: Pennsylvania Department of Education and Department of Public Welfare, Office of Child Development and Early Learning.

Office of Head Start. 2010. *Revisiting and updating the multicultural principles for Head Start programs serving children ages birth to five: Addressing culture and home language in Head Start program systems and services*. Washington, DC: U.S. Department of Health and Human Services, Administration for Children & Families, Office of Head Start.

Paez, M., and Rinaldi, C. 2006. Predicting English word reading skills for Spanish speaking students in first grade. *Topics in Language Disorders 26*(4): 338–350.

Paradis, J., Genesee, F., and Crago, M. B. 2010. *Dual language development & disorders: A handbook on bilingualism & second language learning*, 2nd ed. Baltimore, MD: Paul H. Brookes Publishing.

Pearson, B. Z. 2008. *Raising a bilingual child: A step-by-step guide for parents*. New York: Random House.

Raikes, H. H., and Edwards, C. P. 2009. *Extending the dance in infant & toddler caregiving: Enhancing attachment and relationships*. Baltimore, MD: Paul H. Brookes Publishing.

Raines, S., Miller, K., and Curry-Rood, L. 2002. *Story S-t-r-e-t-c-h-e-r-s for infants, toddlers, and twos: Experiences, activities, and games for popular children's books.* Beltsville, MD: Gryphon House.

Silberg, J. 2009. *Baby smarts: Games for playing and learning.* Beltsville, MD: Gryphon House.

Silberg, J. 2001. *Games to play with babies,* 3rd ed. Beltsville, MD: Gryphon House.

Willis, C. 2009. *Teaching infants, toddlers, and twos with special needs.* Beltsville, MD: Gryphon House.

Wong Fillmore, L. 1991. When learning a second language means losing the first. *Early Childhood Research Quarterly.* 6: 323–346.

Resources

Copple, C., Bredekamp, S., and Gonzalez-Mena, J. 2011. *Basics of developmentally appropriate practice: An introduction of teachers of infants & toddlers.* Washington, DC: National Association for the Education of Young Children.

Dickinson, D. K., and Tabors, P. O., eds. 2001. *Beginning literacy with language: Young children learning at home and school.* Baltimore, MD: Paul H. Brookes Publishing.

Genishi, C. 2009. *Children, language, and literacy: Diverse learners in diverse times.* New York: Teachers College Press.

Hart, B., and Risley, T. R. 1995. *Meaningful differences in the everyday experience of young American children.* Baltimore, MD: Paul H. Brookes Publishing.

Hart B., and Risley, T. R. 1999. *The social world of children learning to talk.* Baltimore, MD: Paul H. Brookes Publishing.

Howes, C. 2009. *Culture and child development in early childhood programs: Practices for quality education and care (early childhood education).* New York: Teachers College Press.

Johnson, J. 2009. *Babies in the rain: Promoting play, exploration, and discovery with infants and toddlers.* St. Paul, MN: Redleaf Press.

Kovach, B., and Da Ros-Voseles, D. 2008. *Being with babies: Understanding and responding to the infants in your care.* Beltsville, MD: Gryphon House.

Miller, M. 1998. *Baby faces.* New York: Little Simon.

Nemeth, K., and Brillante, P. 2011. Solving the puzzle: Dual language learners with challenging behaviors. *Young Children 66*(4): 12–17.

Nemeth, K. 2009. *Many languages, one classroom: Teaching dual and English language learners.* Beltsville, MD: Gryphon House.

Rosenkoetter, S., and Knapp-Philo, J. 2006. *Learning to read the world: Language and literacy in the first three years.* Washington, DC: Zero to Three: National Center for Infants, Toddlers, and Families.

Stechuk, R. A., Burns, M. S., and Yandian, S. E. 2006. *Bilingual infant/toddler environments: Supporting language & learning in our youngest children.* Washington, DC: Academy for Educational Development Center for Early Care and Education.

Tabors, P. O. 2008. *One child, two languages: A guide for early childhood educators of children learning English as a second language,* 2nd ed. Baltimore, MD: Paul H. Brookes Publishing.

U.S. Copyright Office. Fair use. http://www.copyright.gov/fls/fl102.html

Weitzman, E., and Greenberg, J. 2002. *Learning language and loving it: A guide to promoting children's social language and literacy development,* 2nd ed. Toronto: The Hanen Centre.

National Organizations

Colorín Colorado bilingual literacy site: colorincolorado.org

Council for Exceptional Children, Division for Early Childhood: dec-sped.org

Early Head Start National Resource Center: eclkc.ohs.acf.hhs.gov/hslc/tta-system/ehsnrc

National Association for the Education of Young Children: naeyc.org

Zero to Three: ztt.org

Index